THE *Boat* COOKBOOK

REAL FOOD FOR HUNGRY SAILORS

FIONA SIMS

Foreword by Chris Galvin

ADLARD COLES

LONDON · OXFORD · NEW YORK · NEW DELHI · SYDNEY

Big, simple flavours combined brilliantly – inventive,unpretentious and delicious.
HESTON BLUMENTHAL, OBE

Fiona's passion for all things nautical is only eclipsed by her passion
for good food and a glass of wine, preferably at sea. With or without
a boat, Fiona's book is a delicious treat.

MICHEL ROUX JR

Fiona cooks from the heart and her recipes really hit the spot for rustling up
a quick, delicious meal, whether on board or at home.

ANGELA HARTNETT, MBE

It's sometimes difficult to come up with new recipes on board, so a book like
The Boat Cookbook, with its mouthwatering recipes, is a valuable addition to
a boat's bookshelf – you will never be short of crew again!

SIR ROBIN KNOX-JOHNSTON

ADLARD COLES
Bloomsbury Publishing Plc
50 Bedford Square, London, WC1B 3DP, UK

BLOOMSBURY, ADLARD COLES and the Adlard Coles
logo are trademarks of Bloomsbury Publishing Plc

First published in Great Britain 2014
This edition published 2019

A catalogue record for this book is available from the
British Library

Library of Congress Cataloguing-in-Publication data has
been applied for

ISBN: PB: 978-1-4729-6568-4; eBook: 978-1-4729-6569-1

2 4 6 8 10 9 7 5 3 1

Typeset in Leander Regular by Lee-May Lim
Printed and bound in China by Toppan Leefung Printing

Bloomsbury Publishing Plc makes every effort to ensure
that the papers used in the manufacture of our books are
natural, recyclable products made from wood grown in well-
managed forests. Our manufacturing processes conform to
the environmental regulations of the country of origin.

To find out more about our authors and books visit www.
bloomsbury.com and sign up for our newsletters

Photography by Julian Winslow
Illustrations by Louise Sheeran

Note: while all reasonable care has been taken in
the publication of this book, the publisher takes no
responsibility for the use of the methods

Contents

Foreword

Ah, smell the sea air! These were always the first words my nan uttered when we arrived on the Essex coast. You could spot our large family from a mile away, having the biggest picnic on the beach. 'That smell will make you hungry, Chris,' she would say. And she was right: there is just something about the sea that switches our appetites into overdrive.

Sitting on the beach I used to wait patiently for the other highlight of the day: watching out for the Thames barge with its tan sails, ghosting up to the shore. A plank was thrown over the side and a ride around the pier cost half a crown per family. How I dreamt of this trip; in fact, I can honestly say that for nearly fifty years this passage has rarely left my dreams.

I recently took the plunge and bought the boat I fantasised about all those years ago – and of course my focus was quickly drawn to the tiny galley. Having spent a lifetime cooking in some of the best restaurant kitchens, achieving my other childhood dream of attaining a Michelin star, now was the time for me to address my sailing ambitions. And it made perfect sense: to my mind, food and the sea form one of those great natural marriages we chefs are always looking for.

And then there's wine, which is where my special friendship with Fiona began, and how I came to be writing this foreword.

I have always enjoyed reading Fiona's food and wine journalism. All snobbery banished and simply explained, her writing feels like she is leading you by the hand through famous vineyards and legendary kitchens, seeking out those undiscovered grape varieties and local ingredients, and chatting warmly about the qualities of the vine and the passion in the kitchen.

Over the years I have been lucky enough to get to know Fiona as being good as her word, always making people feel welcome at tastings, sharing her wisdom and knowledge; someone who is very democratic in her views and advice, possessing the gift of making you feel that no question is too stupid to ask.

When Fiona told me she was writing this book I thought it was a brilliant idea, and I was even happier when she asked me to contribute a couple of recipes. Having eaten some very odd dishes while on my Competent Crew and Day Skipper courses, I feel that this book will become a much-loved and essential part of any sailor's library, next to their almanacs and pilot guides.

Inside these covers, Fiona has included her personal favourites, and has also managed to persuade a treasure trove of British sailors and top restaurant chefs to contribute generously, creating and sharing some of their own recipes, making this book a very special collection of inspirational and achievable ideas.

Whether a beginner in the galley or a more experienced cook, you cannot fail to improve your food on board after reading this. And even with the tiniest galley, it will provide ideas for you to be able to sail in style. Anchoring for a lunch of fish stew with gremolata couldn't be simpler or more delicious, and will soon make you a very happy crew indeed.

Fiona has chosen these dishes like her wines, with a discerning eye. The book is simply arranged into sections that are easy to reference: Galley, In Harbour, At Sea, At Home and Booze. When I received the first draft of the recipes they looked balanced, delicious and begging to be cooked, but most importantly they take into consideration the disciplines needed to cook on board – lamb with sumac and butter-bean mash has already become a favourite with my family without leaving the shore.

There really is something for everyone to try and enough scope for you to really spoil yourself and your crew the next time you are on board. I hope you enjoy this book as much as I intend to – happy cooking!

Chris Galvin
Chef Patron, Galvin Restaurants

Introduction

You can blame my dad for this book. He kept losing the scribbled-down recipes that I gave him to improve his basic cooking skills. The few he has managed to remember have perked up his menu and he now whips up penne with sardines, fennel and pine nuts in place of tinned Bolognese, and does a mean lamb and artichoke tagine with lemon couscous instead of packet beef stew and powdered mash. So now there's no excuse for any sailor stuck on a tin treadmill.

When I sail with Dad, that's another matter. I arrive on board laden with fresh herbs destined for a salad, or warm frittata that I made at home earlier; a tin of my own flapjacks tucked under my arm to keep us going through the day. If we're away overnight, then my bag is stashed with goodies to rustle up supper and breakfast. For longer forays, harbour shops are eagerly anticipated, with the best produce sought out after some brazen quizzing of locals.

This book might be useful to those on long ocean crossings, but really it's intended for people, like me, who sail at weekends, either around their own coasts, or to nearby countries. And it's for those who like to spend their holidays on boats, and others who have time for longer, more leisurely cruises, putting into port on a regular basis. Not forgetting those of you who might dream of a life on the water but prefer to stay firmly on land – these recipes also work for the time-strapped cook with limited equipment but a yearning for big flavours.

The eighty-odd recipes are mostly mine, with the rest borrowed – five from world-record-breaking yachtsmen and women, who generously shared their galley secrets (including a gloriously trashy tortilla pizza – thanks, Dee Caffari), and another five from top British chefs, who gave their elegant recipes a suitably nautical spin: mackerel tartare, anyone?

Most of the dishes can be completed in 20–30 minutes tops, and most are enough for four hungry sailors, though a few dishes are for two (they just work better that way on board). Virtually all the ingredients are available at the supermarket, and where they aren't, I've included online contact details.

There are five sections in all, starting with Galley, which includes advice on kit to buy and ingredients to stash. It's followed by In Harbour, which focuses on dishes to be enjoyed with only a quick row from a mooring to the shops, allowing you to spend a little longer in the galley. Then At Sea, for when you want to rustle up something quick and sustaining but always delicious; and At Home, for all those boat essentials that can be cooked in advance. Finally, but no less importantly, Booze, because we know a sailor likes a drink. But while posh wines are great, plonk can be good – even plonk in wine boxes – and wine boxes so work on boats, with some good ones out there now.

There are a few indulgences in the book – white truffle oil being the most outrageous (wicked sprinkled on popcorn). And I hold my hand up to using certain ingredients to excess – notably Parmesan, extra virgin olive oil, fresh herbs, nuts and copious vegetables. I love meat and I eat a lot of fish, but I love vegetables more.

And there we are. Now heave to and fire up that stove!

'Bad cooking is responsible for more trouble at sea than all other things put together.'

Thomas Fleming Day, yacht designer and founder editor of *Rudder* magazine (1861–1927)

Galley

If you're reading this on a large motor-cruiser or swanky yacht, then you've probably got a better kitchen on board than mine at home. This hit list isn't for you. I'm talking to those of you who have a modest galley – one up from a camper van, and two up from a camping stove. I'm thinking cool box, and if you're really lucky a refrigerator, a two-ring hob, a postbox-size grill and a Wendy house of an oven (we use a Neptune 4500).

Space really is at a premium and everything has its place, so the kit you choose should be carefully selected. Pots and pans should stack easily, and dishes should be both oven- and table-friendly. There are lots of space-saving options around, so take advantage of the latest clever kitchenware.

If you're not a tidy freak in everyday life, then you certainly need to be on board. Once you've worked out what recipes you are likely to be cooking, store ingredients to hand and know what's where.

A galley to be proud of

It's a good idea to keep a master list of everything you stash on board, then every time you finish something, cross it off so you remember to replace it the next time you shop. And if you're being this organised, you might as well date stamp your supplies, to avoid that sawdust spice moment. Ideally, it's healthier and cheaper to buy as you go, keeping only basic items such as flour, sugar, cereals and store-cupboard staples on board for when you're caught short, or just can't be bothered.

I'm not suggesting that you stock up on all the things I've listed – it's just to give you a few ideas, and to encourage you to break free from the treadmill of everyday ingredients now and then by discovering something new.

Take ras el hanout. This wonderfully complex Moroccan spice – now in a supermarket near you – is the reason why a humble cut of lamb can taste sensational. And I'm having a love affair with sumac – I'm rubbing it over everything, from fish fillets to juicy chops, its addictive lemony tang a great substitute for the fresh fruit if you find yourself lacking.

Always have a store-cupboard supper or two stashed away for when you arrive too late for the shops, or can't get ashore. If you're missing an ingredient, be brave and substitute another. And never underestimate the power of comfort food – stock up on sweet treats.

Wave Wisdom
TAKE-ON-BOARD BASICS

Sourdough bread (because it tastes good and lasts so long – see page 25), eggs, milk, butter, Parmesan, feta, lemon, garlic bulb, fresh herbs, chorizo, onion.

Kit

BAKING TIN – one that fits your oven size exactly; non-stick helps. Roasting bags are another useful addition.

BARBECUE – if you're fed up with being stuck in the galley on hot summer evenings, consider a boat barbecue – charcoal, of course. Though many a sailor is nervous about flames near fibreglass, so you might prefer to opt for a portable barbecue to use at the beach instead.

CHOPPING BOARDS – ideally choose several flexible, colour-coded, synthetic ones, so you avoid any cross-contamination when chopping raw meat and fish. I buy mine from innovative British kitchenware designer Joseph Joseph (www.josephjoseph.com).

COCKTAIL SHAKER – don't laugh. Essential if you love a cocktail on board. Unbreakable, too, if you choose a stainless steel one, though you can of course improvise and use a Thermos.

COLANDER – stainless steel is best, though if you can be trusted to keep a plastic one away from the hob, consider Joseph Joseph's space-saving folding one.

CONTAINERS – decant your coffee, tea and sugar into durable containers, keeping clear of glass; re-use and top up supermarket jars of herbs and spices.

CUTLERY – the usual set of knives, forks and spoons, plus a wooden spoon, fish slice, scissors, bottle and can openers, vegetable peeler, lemon zester, small balloon whisk, grater (Microplane is a good make), and skewers.

HERB SAVER – unless otherwise mentioned, whenever I refer to herbs in the book I'm talking fresh herbs. Dried herbs generally require longer cooking times, though there are exceptions – namely oregano, thyme, rosemary and bay leaves. And before you say, 'And just how do you expect us to keep herbs fresh on board?' I give you the Prepara Mini Herb Saver Pod, available from www.whiskcooking.co.uk – better than bunging them in a glass of water to keep them fresh. They will keep for up to two weeks in the pod in a conventional fridge, and for a few days in a cool box.

KETTLE – choose one you can fill through the spout – it's easier.

KNIVES – buy good ones, keep them sharp and store them safely; it will make life on board easier and cut down on preparation times. A 13cm cook's knife should see you through most jobs, plus a smaller paring knife for fiddly jobs. And if you are going to take advantage of the sea's bountiful produce, then you'll also need a fish-boning knife and an oyster knife.

MANDOLIN – sounds a bit poncy, I know, but you can buy a cheap version of this slicer (OXO Good Grips does a good-value plastic one) and it will make salads more exciting.

MEASURING CUPS/JUG – buy separately or with mixing bowls (see page 12). Failing that, use a standard mug – it should hold about 225ml of liquid or enough rice for two to three people. Or just guess, which I do frequently, with varying accuracy.

MIXING BOWLS – you will need a couple. Best is a set of stainless steel mixing bowls that will fit inside the pressure cooker for easy storage. Even better if it comes with integrated measuring cups.

OVEN THERMOMETER – because many galley stoves are difficult to regulate and thermostats are often unreliable.

POTS AND PANS – one deep-sided sauté pan with a lid ideally around 28cm in diameter, plus a smaller saucepan, both preferably with removable handles for easy storage. Don't stint on your pans. They should be made of stainless steel and have thick bottoms – even heat distribution is the name of the game here. You'll also need a couple of less durable but cheaper non-stick frying pans – far easier on the washing-up – which you can bin when the surfaces are worn.

PRESSURE COOKER – it's your fastest route to a sustaining meal on the boat, transforming dried beans into soups and stews in just 20 minutes. It saves on fuel, too, and survives happily during an errant wake. Invest in a good one – the pans should be made from stainless steel (see page 13). In fact, a fair number of the recipes in this book could be cooked more quickly in a pressure cooker, but I've singled out four as being particularly pressure-cooker-friendly. The pressure cooker also doubles up as a pasta pan, or indeed any time you need to use a deep saucepan – just find another lid for it. Deep pans are particularly good when the waves start rolling the boat.

RAMEKINS – sure, you can make one big dish, but dividing the recipes up into individual portion sizes not only cuts down the cooking time, they double up as serving dishes too, so less washing-up. Use metal ones on board.

 *Wave Wisdom*

Measure the top of your hob first and check that the pans will be able to sit together in most combinations.

SPLATTER GUARD – because the last thing you want in a confined space is smelly grease splats.

SMOKER – you can buy compact hot-smokers these days, or make your own – though filling the cabin full of smoke isn't ideal, so keep the smoker for use at the beach or at home for making the most of your catch after a trip (see page 120).

TABLEWARE – plastic is the way to go on board when it comes to boat tableware, but that doesn't mean it can't be stylish. There are plenty of brands out there (I'm also particularly partial to the blue-edged white enamelware from www.falconenamelware.com). Make sure you include deep-dished bowls for porridge, soups and noodles. Choose stackable drinking tumblers to save on space.

THERMOS – for keeping those hot dogs at the ready, for keeping soup warm for when you need it, for shaking a cocktail, and for a supply of hot drinks during a night watch.

WEIGHING SCALES – you can just guess, of course (it gets better with practice), but if you would rather play it safe then buy some folding digital scales – try www.josephjoseph.com.

 *Wave Wisdom*

Silica gel – moisture is your enemy no more with these clever little packs, which you can stash in storage jars as a desiccant to control humidity and avoid spoilage (just don't eat it).

Learn to love your pressure cooker

It's one of life's great time-savers, the pressure cooker. It's a fuel saver, too, and that means a lot on a boat. Pressure-cooking preserves more vitamins, minerals, colour and aroma in your food than any other method of cooking. I'm not a big fan of kitchen gadgets as a rule, but the pressure cooker has opened my eyes. After years in the culinary doldrums it's now back in favour, thanks, in part, to the economic downturn that had us all seeking out cheaper cuts of meat and the best ways to cook them. The pressure cooker also makes light work of rice, pulses and some puddings.

But forget the hissing, fizzing pots of old – the new generation are made of sleek, sturdy stainless steel and are safer and easier to use. I love Kuhn Rikon's Duromatic (available from www.lakeland.co.uk). We're talking goulash in 30 minutes, a pot of soft chickpeas in 10 minutes, and risotto in 5 minutes. If you want to save on water on board, you can vent naturally and add another 20 minutes to the total cooking time.

There's a bit of trial and error involved, working through watery gravies and mushy veg, but beef shin and lamb neck will never taste so good, and there are some excellent books around to guide you, such as Richard Ehrlich's *80 Recipes for your Pressure Cooker* (Kyle Cathie), and *The Pressure Cooker Cookbook* by Catherine Phipps (Ebury).

LITTLE TIP

'Cook in a pressure cooker. It saves fuel, but its greatest advantage is that if the boat lurches, and the lid is on properly when it falls from the stove, the contents don't go all over the cabin.' Sir Robin Knox-Johnston, sailor

Locker

I'm not suggesting that you stock all of the below – these are just to give you an idea of the sorts of ingredients that work well on board. And some of them you will need for the recipes that follow.

BAKING INGREDIENTS – plain flour, baking powder, caster sugar.

CEREALS – jumbo porridge oats, homemade granola (see page 117).

GRAINS AND PULSES – pearled spelt (it cooks faster than barley and it's nuttier, too), basmati rice, quinoa, couscous, Puy lentils, red lentils, quick-cook polenta.

HERBS, SPICES, SALT AND PEPPER – smoked paprika (it gives a meaty depth to soups and stews), ras el hanout (this Moroccan blend is the spice mix du jour), sumac (try rubbing it on a lamb chop), curry powder, garam masala, cinnamon, thyme, rosemary, ginger, crushed chillies, cumin, coriander, turmeric, fennel seeds, nutmeg, bay leaves, bouquets garnis, saffron, black pepper, sea salt (when I list salt in the recipes, I mean sea salt rather than table salt, and Maldon is particularly good).

HOT DRINKS – tea bags (including herbal), ground and instant coffee, cocoa powder, and powdered and UHT milk.

NUTS, SEEDS AND DRIED FRUIT – including almonds, walnuts, pine nuts, cashews, pistachios, peanuts, mixed seed sprinkle, dried apricots, prunes and sultanas.

OILS AND VINEGARS – when I list olive or rapeseed oil in the recipes I'm talking extra virgin, which I use in pretty much everything – rapeseed increasingly as it's British, cheaper, healthier and tastes almost as good as anything from Tuscany. But if that's too extravagant, reserve the extra virgin olive oil for drizzling and stock up on bog-standard olive oil for the rest. Also stock balsamic and white wine vinegar.

ODDS AND ENDS – dried porcini (tart up ordinary mushrooms and add to soups and stews), sun-dried tomatoes, tofu (it comes in a small handy box with a long shelf life and an ingenious ability to sop up flavours and keep you healthy), maple syrup, 70% dark chocolate.

OLIVES AND PICKLES – go for superior olives (preferably those packed in extra virgin olive oil), jalapeño peppers (hot dogs will never be the same again), capers, 'lazy' chilli (the ready-prepared stuff that comes in jars stored in vinegar is the only 'lazy' ingredient that I rate, but the garlic equivalent is pretty heinous), or if you prefer fresh chilli, then keep some rubber gloves aside just for chopping chillies to avoid any uncomfortable mishaps.

PRESERVES AND SPREADS – marmalade, honey, Marmite, peanut butter, Nutella, salted caramel sauce (the last two are seriously addictive stirred into yoghurt for an instant dessert).

Wave Wisdom

THE PERFECT VINAIGRETTE

In a screwtop jar, combine 2 teaspoons Dijon mustard, 2 tablespoons red or white wine vinegar, 6 tablespoons olive or rapeseed oil, 1 tsp honey and a pinch of salt. Shake until emulsified. Store in the fridge or cool box until needed.

RICE, PASTA AND NOODLES – basmati rice, risotto rice, angel's hair pasta, macaroni, orzo, penne, spaghetti, egg noodles, rice noodles, udon noodles.

SAUCES AND PASTES – horseradish, hot chilli, ketchup, mayonnaise (Benedicta is good), mustard (Maille Dijon is a favourite), passata, pesto, soy, salsa, Tabasco, tomato sauce, Worcestershire sauce, laksa, miso, tapenade, tomato paste.

STOCK – Marigold vegetable bouillon; look no further.

TINS AND PACKETS – anchovies, baked beans, beef consommé, chickpeas, chopped tomatoes, tomato soup (Heinz, naturally), coconut milk, corned beef, duck confit, pâté, tuna, sardine fillets, white crabmeat, artichoke hearts, prunes, chickpeas, butter beans, cannellini beans, borlotti beans, haricot beans, evaporated milk (makes deliciously creamy porridge, see page 22), vacuum-packed wholemeal pitta bread, vacuum-packed wholemeal flour tortillas, long-life fruit juice, popping corn.

Four great spice mixes

Save time and shelf life by making up your own mix for fish and meat, for easy, flavour-packed grilling. Store in small airtight containers for up to three months.

Spice Mix No. 1

Perfect for tagines and all things Moroccan.

2 tbsp ground coriander
1 tbsp paprika
1 tbsp ground ginger
1 tbsp ground cumin
2 tsp ground cinnamon
1 tsp cayenne pepper
1 tsp ground allspice
½ tsp ground cloves
1 tsp salt
½ tsp ground black pepper

Spice Mix No. 2

Transform supermarket chicken with this aromatic rub.

2 tbsp ground cumin
1 tbsp ground coriander
1 tbsp ground cinnamon
1 tsp dried thyme
1 tsp smoked paprika
1 tsp garlic granules
1 tsp salt
½ tsp ground black pepper

Spice Mix No. 3

An Italian sauce seasoning for when standing in the galley doesn't appeal.

3 tbsp dried basil

3 tbsp dried oregano

3 tbsp dried marjoram

1 tsp dried thyme

1 tsp dried rosemary

¼ tsp ground black pepper

¼ tsp crushed dried chillies

1 tbsp garlic granules

1 tsp onion powder

1 tsp salt

Spice Mix No. 4

Great as a barbecue rub on oily fish fillets.

1 tbsp dark brown sugar

1 tbsp ground cumin

1 tbsp dried thyme

1 tsp ground black pepper

1 tsp smoked paprika

1 tsp chilli powder (mild)

1 tsp cinnamon

1 tsp salt

~ Wave Wisdom
INGREDIENTS YOU MIGHT NOT BE FAMILIAR WITH

Today's supermarket shelves are groaning with products from the furthest corners of the globe, and I take full advantage of this exotic booty. I'm not sure where my life would be without sumac, the Middle Eastern spice with its lemony tang that livens up salads, meat and fish with just a pinch. And I haven't looked back since I spiked a lamb tagine with Moroccan rose petal-flecked ras el hanout. Salads just got a whole lot more interesting with nutty, ancient grain spelt, and I have the Incas to thank for quinoa, which has become an impressively healthy addition to my store cupboard. On a cold day, a slick of Singaporean laksa paste stirred into a bowl of hot noodles will warm the cockles; and I've ditched the cup-a-soup for a bowl of instant miso: just as comforting and healthier, too.

out at sea

BACK IN THE DAY

Egyptian sailors liked to carry a flat brittle loaf of maize bread called 'dhourra' cake. The Romans preferred to munch on a biscuit called 'buccellum'. And when Richard the Lionheart sailed off on his Third Crusade, he took with him a 'biskit of muslin' – a medley of barley, rye and bean flour.

Jump forward to the eighteenth century and a seaman's supper would have consisted largely of ship's biscuit, salted meat and lots of booze. There were other ingredients that livened things up, such as dried peas, oatmeal, pork, butter and cheese – though only if you were a naval man.

Your regular merchant seaman wasn't quite so lucky. Salted meat stayed in the cask for years at a stretch until it was so hard that it looked like wood. And bread was full of weevils – the sailors used to tap it on the table before eating to frighten the critters out. But you can see the logistical problems: provisions had to be moved over long distances, at a time when it took six weeks to reach the Mediterranean and up to six months to get to India.

The ship's biscuit took centre stage on the boat table right up until the introduction of tinned food in 1813. To make a ship's biscuit, add water to a pound of wholemeal flour and a good pinch of salt to make a stiff dough, leave it for 30 minutes, and then roll out thickly to make six biscuits. Bake in a hot oven for 30 minutes and leave to harden in a warm, dry atmosphere. Or you could just buy a packet of Carr's Table Water biscuits, the modern-day equivalent.

In Harbour

The more adventurous boat cooking takes place in harbour. There's nothing better than grabbing a mooring and setting off to explore a town in search of good food.

I have no shame. If there's no harbour master available to quiz, I tap up bank clerks and shop owners, hairdressers and chandlers for their favourite places to buy food in town. Are there any good bakers? What's the butcher like? Who is supplying the best fresh fish? And I visibly quiver at the sight of a farmers' market. The aim, as at home, is to buy the best I can – even when it comes to tins. Weighed down with my finds, I return to the boat eager to get cooking.

Plump, fresh mussels hit the pot with a few slugs of locally produced farmhouse cider. Carefully picked dressed crab is folded into macaroni cheese, elevating this everyday dish to something classy. Puffed and golden red chilli-flecked sweetcorn fritters slide out of the pan to accompany grilled fresh trout. Mackerel that we caught en route is filleted and combined with cucumber and fresh tarragon. Best butcher's sausages are torn into chunks and simmered in a rich tomato ragù before being sopped up with a cheese-laced polenta. Fat cherries are suspended in a blanket of crisp, light sweetened batter.

Don't know how to fillet a fish? Then I've included a step-by-step guide (see pages 42–43). The more you practise, the better you'll get. Just remember to buy a good fish-boning knife. Unexpected guests? No problem. Home in on locker-friendly dishes, such as sumac, quinoa, lentil and green bean salad (page 37), or just bump up volumes by throwing in a few extra handfuls of store-cupboard staples.

And don't forget about the rest of the free food that's out there for the taking. In the late summer, bramble bushes are groaning with fruit – add them to breakfast and desserts, or save them for a hedgerow brûlée later at sea (see page 112). In the spring, pathways are lined with wild garlic, which will liven up eggs a treat. And from June to September, shorelines deliver crunchy samphire, a perfect partner for grilled fish (see page 60).

Apricot and pecan cream porridge

Forget tinned cream – I've taken to drizzling evaporated milk on to my porridge even when I'm not on board. When combined with cinnamon and honey it tastes pretty luxurious and will set you up for the day. Try substituting prunes for the apricots – and when you have access, fresh soft fruits like blueberries, raspberries and strawberries also work a treat.

For 4
160g rolled jumbo oats
handful of dried, ready-to-eat apricots, chopped
1.2 litres cold water
100ml evaporated milk
1 tsp cinnamon
pinch of salt

To serve:
handful of pecan nuts, toasted and chopped
2 extra apricots, chopped
4 tbsp honey or maple syrup

Add the oats and apricots to a saucepan with the water and simmer for 6 minutes, stirring frequently. Meanwhile, toast the pecan nuts in a baking tin under the grill for 3–4 minutes, turning them once before setting aside to roughly chop when cool enough to handle. When the porridge is cooked, stir in the evaporated milk, cinnamon and salt and serve immediately, sprinkled with the toasted pecans, extra chopped apricots and drizzled honey or maple syrup.

 *Wave Wisdom*

FIVE GREAT WEATHER PROVERBS

Red sky at night, shepherds' delight; red sky in the morning, shepherds' warning.

Halo around the sun or moon, rain or snow is coming soon.

One swallow does not a summer make.

Rain before seven, fine by eleven.

The sudden storm lasts not three hours.

Cinnamon honey figs with ricotta and toasted almonds

I'd happily eat this for breakfast (minus the rum) as well as for dessert (with the rum). Figs, honey and ricotta is just one of those perfect combinations. Figs are plentiful in the late summer months, and while they are delicate when ripe, the softer they are the better they taste.

For 4
2 tbsp flaked almonds
1 tbsp butter
8 ripe figs
splash of rum, or orange juice
1 tsp ground cinnamon
4 tbsp runny honey
250g ricotta cheese

Preheat the grill. In a small baking tin, toast the almonds under the grill until golden, about 2–3 minutes, turning once. Tip out and set aside. Lightly grease the tin with a bit of the butter. Cut the figs in half lengthways and put them cut side up in the tin, dot with the remaining butter, sprinkle with the rum (or orange juice) and the cinnamon and grill for 5 minutes until the figs are softened. Drizzle with the honey and divide the ricotta between 4 bowls. Top with the figs, spooning their juices over, and scatter with toasted almonds.

Porcini on toast with eggs

Shop-bought mushrooms can sometimes lack flavour, but combine them with some dried porcini and hey presto, you have an intense mushroomy hit. This makes a great breakfast, lunch or supper dish – just remember to use good free-range eggs.

For 4
1 tbsp olive or rapeseed oil
30g dried porcini, soaked in a little warm water for 20 minutes and drained
500g large flat mushrooms, wiped and sliced
1 garlic clove, peeled and crushed
½ tsp dried thyme
2 tbsp butter
4 large free-range eggs
4 thick slices of sourdough bread
salt and pepper

To serve:
small handful of parsley, chopped (optional)

Heat the oil in a frying pan. Add the dried and fresh mushrooms, garlic and thyme and cook for 5 minutes until soft, then season, remove from the pan and keep warm. Melt 2 teaspoons of butter in the frying pan then break the eggs into it and fry until the whites are set and the yolks still slightly runny. Meanwhile, heat the grill and toast the bread, then slather with the rest of the butter. Divide the warm mushrooms between the slices of toast and top with a fried egg, another grind of salt and pepper, and a garnish of chopped parsley.

THE SECRET OF SOURDOUGH

With its six-day shelf life, sourdough bread is the way to go on board. Sourdough is the original method of producing leavened bread – and some argue it's still the best. Naturally occurring (sometimes called wild) yeasts are less concentrated than commercial yeasts, so sourdough can be good for people who react badly to excessive yeast in bread. Wild yeasts ferment more slowly, allowing time for beneficial bacteria to develop, which contributes to the flavour and slows up the staling of the loaf. To find out who bakes your nearest sourdough loaf, visit the Real Bread Campaign at www.sustainweb.org/realbread and use its Bread Finder. Or make your starter and bake your own, with a little help from books such as *Bread Matters* by Andrew Whitley (Fourth Estate), who also runs bread-making courses at www.breadmatters.com.

Chris Galvin's
Piperade basquaise 👨‍🍳

I've eaten this for breakfast, lunch and supper; such is the flexible appeal of this Basque classic – essentially scrambled eggs with a red pepper and onion marmalade. This version is courtesy of sailing-mad chef Chris Galvin, a multi-Michelin-starred chef with five restaurants in the capital, two in Edinburgh, two in Dubai and a gastropub in Essex. You need to make his marmalade first (see page 127), which could be done on board, but to save time and fuel it's best to make it at home. Then all you need to do is stir it into scrambled eggs and garnish with croutons. You could also add grilled-until-crispy air-dried ham.

For 4

For the croutons:
2 tbsp olive oil
4 slices of sourdough bread (or half a ciabatta), crusts removed, diced into 1cm cubes
pinch of sea salt

For the eggs:
25g butter
8 medium free-range eggs, beaten with a little seasoning
1 quantity red pepper and onion marmalade (see page 127)
salt and pepper

To serve:
handful of flat-leaf parsley, roughly chopped

First make the croutons. Toss the oil and bread cubes together in a bowl with the sea salt. Tip into a non-stick frying pan and gently toast, tossing from time to time to get an even colour. Set aside. Wipe the pan clean, then put back on the hob and melt the butter. Turn up the heat and add the eggs, stirring all the time. Once the eggs just begin to thicken and gently scramble, stir in the marmalade. Continue to stir, making sure the eggs are kept creamy. Once a very soft scrambled egg is achieved, remove from the pan and divide between the plates. To finish, top with the croutons and parsley.

Things on toast

An instant breakfast, lunch, supper or superior snack — there's all sorts you can pile on to a slice of toasted bread (sourdough, preferably — see page 25):

- cream cheese dusted with cinnamon and drizzled with honey

- prosciutto and asparagus — I often use fat, white, Spanish Navarrico asparagus that come in jars from www.brindisa.com (a brilliant source of lots of toast toppings, from piquillo peppers to Cantabrian anchovies)

- tinned artichoke hearts, mozzarella and stoned black olives

- purple sprouting broccoli boiled until tender, with toasted pine nuts and goats' cheese

- whole cherry tomatoes roasted with garlic and combined with tinned butter beans and a few drops of balsamic vinegar, olive oil and basil

- fresh white crabmeat strewn over slices of tomato topped with chopped chives

- grilled courgette with feta cheese and chopped fresh mint

- a dollop of horseradish stirred into grated Cheddar and melted under the grill

- shucked, chopped fresh oysters mixed with pan-fried bacon and a scattering of flat-leaf parsley

- ripe avocados mashed with crushed dried chilli flakes and a drizzle of olive oil.

Crab toasts with tomato salad

Crab and tomato is just one of those perfect pairings. The addition of semi-dried tomatoes (a useful store-cupboard staple) to the accompanying salad will sweeten up any store-bought tomatoes that might fall a bit short in the flavour department. For more topping ideas for toasted bread, see page 27.

For 2

handful of cherry tomatoes, halved

1 tbsp semi-dried tomatoes in olive oil, halved

1 tbsp spring onions, trimmed and chopped

handful of basil leaves, torn

1 dressed crab, or tinned white crabmeat

2 hard-boiled eggs, shelled and chopped

juice of ¼ lemon

2 tbsp mayonnaise

2 slices of sourdough bread, toasted

salt and pepper

Combine both fresh and dried tomatoes in a bowl, nicking a little bit of the spring onions and torn basil to mix through, and season to taste. Place the crabmeat in another bowl, and mix in the rest of the spring onions and basil, the hard-boiled eggs, the lemon juice and the mayonnaise. Season to taste again, then pile it on to the toasted sourdough. Serve with the tomato salad.

Ed Wilson's mackerel tartare, cucumber and tarragon

Chef Ed Wilson loves nothing more than fresh, quality ingredients cooked simply, and you'll find him at his celebrated East London restaurant, Brawn. This is his answer to the copious quantities of mackerel caught on sailing trips – a very simple but elegant preparation that relies entirely on the freshness of the fish, so don't try this at home unless the fish is super-fresh. He suggests poshing it up further with two chopped king scallops, which you've prised out of their shells. No cooking, little preparation, just a good knife and chopping board required.

For 2

500g mackerel, preferably plucked straight from the ocean, gutted, filleted, skinned and fine bones removed (see pages 42–43)
½ cucumber
extra virgin olive oil, to taste
20 fresh tarragon leaves, chopped
pinch of sea salt, crushed

To serve:
crusty bread

Using a sharp knife, cut the skinned mackerel fillets into dice roughly the size of your small fingernail. Peel the cucumber and cut it lengthways, scooping out the seeds with a teaspoon, and dice the same way as the fish. In a mixing bowl, combine the diced mackerel and cucumber. Season with crushed sea salt and add olive oil to taste. To serve, divide the tartare equally between two plates and spread out evenly. Sprinkle the chopped tarragon leaves over the top and serve with bread.

Wave Wisdom

HOW TO CATCH A MACKEREL

No boat should be without a mackerel line – with its spinners or feathered hooks it can snare mackerel by the dozen, like taking candy from a baby. Simply unwind the line from the stern, making sure you're not sailing too fast, wait 10 minutes, then reel her in, and repeat until you get lucky. To kill your fish, try a fast blow to the head with the winch handle, then gut by inserting a knife in the bottom of the fish near the tail and draw forwards. Scoop everything out of the cavity and rinse. The best way to enjoy freshly caught mackerel? Eat it raw – like this!

Sausages with Parmesan polenta

Forget sausage and mash, sausage and polenta is the way to go on board – it will satisfy even the hungriest sailor. Just make sure you buy decent sausages (the higher the meat content, the better the quality). If you want a veggie version, this works well with large field mushrooms, sliced up and pan-fried for a few minutes with the onions before adding the tomatoes.

For 4

1 tbsp olive or rapeseed oil
1 large onion, peeled and chopped
8 good quality pork sausages, skinned and cut into 2cm pieces
1 garlic clove, peeled and crushed
2 x 400g tins chopped tomatoes
250ml water
½ tsp chilli flakes
½ tsp dried oregano
300g quick-cook polenta
150g Parmesan cheese, grated
100g unsalted butter
salt and pepper

Heat the oil and soften the onion in a pan. Add the sausage bits and brown them, then add the garlic and soften for a minute or two. Add the tomatoes, water, chillies and oregano, and cook uncovered for 15 minutes. Meanwhile, in another pan, bring 1.5 litres water to the boil. Pour in the polenta slowly and cook, stirring constantly, for 5 minutes or so. Stir in the cheese and butter until well combined. Season and serve, dividing the polenta between 4 dishes and spooning the sausage sauce over.

Grilled gurnard with tapenade, potatoes and spinach

I'm a big fan of gurnard. OK, so it looks a bit prehistoric, but it's lean, firm, white-fleshed and sustainable. It can also take big flavours, and you don't get much bigger than tapenade. I'm not suggesting you make your own on board as there are plenty of good ones available to buy ready-made, but you could make up a batch ahead and it will happily keep in the fridge for a couple of weeks until you need it.

For 4
500g waxy potatoes, peeled
500g spinach leaves, ready-washed
2 tbsp olive or rapeseed oil
4 gurnard fillets (or other white fish fillets)
2 tbsp black olive tapenade
1 lemon, quartered
salt and pepper

Bring a large saucepan of salted water to the boil and cook the potatoes. Drain and keep warm. Place the spinach leaves and a couple of tablespoons of water in that same saucepan, cover and wilt for 2 minutes, then drain and keep warm. Heat the grill to medium. Rub 1 tablespoon of oil on the fish and season. Grill each side for 2–3 minutes, or until cooked through. Divide the potatoes between 4 dishes and cut them into thick slices. Dress with the remaining oil and season. Divide the drained spinach between each dish. Top with the cooked gurnard, spoon the tapenade over and serve with the lemon quarters.

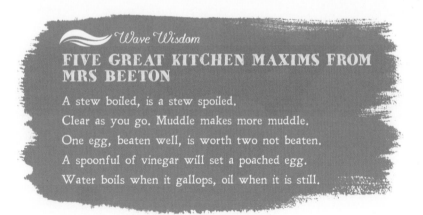

Wave Wisdom
FIVE GREAT KITCHEN MAXIMS FROM MRS BEETON

A stew boiled, is a stew spoiled.
Clear as you go. Muddle makes more muddle.
One egg, beaten well, is worth two not beaten.
A spoonful of vinegar will set a poached egg.
Water boils when it gallops, oil when it is still.

Mussels with cider

This is my take on a classic moules marinière– and more refreshing than the original. The sweetness of the cider works with the briny juiciness of the mussels. Get the fishmonger to remove the beards for you, and cook them soon after you get on board.

For 2
1 tbsp olive or rapeseed oil
1 shallot, peeled and sliced
2 garlic cloves, peeled and crushed
1 bay leaf
grated zest and juice of 1 lemon
1 tbsp brandy (optional)
200ml dry cider
1 kg mussels, washed, beards removed (discard any that are open)
handful of flat-leaf parsley, chopped
salt and pepper

To serve:
crusty bread

Heat the oil in a large, deep pan. Add the shallot, garlic, bay leaf, lemon zest and seasoning, and cook for 2–3 minutes until softened. Add the brandy, if you're using it, and cook until the liquid has evaporated. Pour in the cider and let it boil for a minute or two to let the alcohol burn off. Add the mussels and give it all a good stir. Cover with a lid to let the mussels steam and cook for 3–4 minutes until the shells have opened, giving the pan a good shake every now and again. Discard any that do not open. Add the lemon juice, parsley and a grind of pepper, stir well and serve in deep bowls with crusty bread.

French bean, courgette and blue cheese salad with walnuts

This combines two of my favourite vegetables and it only takes a few minutes to make. You can experiment with the blue cheese but, having tried most of them – from St Agur to Stilton – I think that Roquefort takes the lead thanks to its creamy, salty tang and crumbly texture. When I'm feeling healthy these courgette strips also double up as 'tagliatelle' – try them with a meat ragù or a tomato sauce.

For 4
125g walnuts
250g French beans, topped and tailed
250g courgettes
250g blue cheese, crumbled

For the dressing:
3 tbsp olive or rapeseed oil
1 tbsp balsamic vinegar
1 garlic clove, peeled and crushed
salt and pepper

Toast the walnuts in a frying pan, or in the oven for a few minutes until lightly browned. Let them cool, then roughly chop. Blanch the beans in boiling water for a couple of minutes then rinse in cold water. Shave the courgettes into strips with a wide-bladed vegetable peeler. Mix the dressing ingredients and season. Toss the beans, courgettes and dressing together. Arrange on plates and scatter the crumbled blue cheese and the chopped walnuts over, adding a final grind of black pepper.

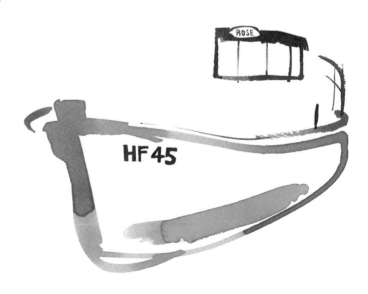

ROSE

HF 45

Spice-rubbed mackerel fillets with sumac, quinoa, lentil and green bean salad

Mackerel can take a bit of spice. And this spice rub, packed with Middle Eastern flavours (see page 17), is one of many you can use. If you can't get fresh mackerel fillets, try smoked mackerel instead, or any other meaty fish. The salad is good on its own, too, and can be dressed up with lots of different vegetables – in which case try adding crumbled feta cheese to make it more substantial. The combination of sumac, quinoa and lentils is a revelation, introduced to me by award-winning chef, food writer and cookery teacher Sabrina Ghayour, one of the strongest voices in Middle Eastern food today, and it now makes a regular appearance at home and in the galley.

For 4

125g Puy lentils

100g quinoa

250g green beans, topped and tailed and chopped in half

handful of flat-leaf parsley, finely chopped

handful of mint, finely chopped

1 bunch of spring onions, trimmed and thinly sliced

4 tbsp olive or rapeseed oil

3 lemons

1 tsp sumac

Spice Mix No. 1, to taste (see page 17)

4 mackerel, filleted (see pages 44–45)

salt and pepper

Rinse the lentils and place in a saucepan with triple the volume of cold water. Bring to the boil and simmer for 10 minutes before adding the quinoa. Bring to the boil and simmer for 10 minutes before adding the chopped green beans. After 5 minutes drain the mixture thoroughly and place in a large bowl. Add the herbs, spring onions, olive oil and the juice of 2 of the lemons, along with the sumac. Season and give it a good stir.

Rub ¼ teaspoon of the spice mixture into each side of your fish fillets, followed by a quick brush of olive oil. Heat your grill or griddle pan and cook the fillets for 2–3 minutes each side until done. Serve with the sumac salad and a lemon quarter each.

Cod, chorizo and chickpea stew

Chorizo is a sailor's best friend. It keeps for ages, it's widely available, and a little goes a long way, adding depth of flavour to everything. There are so many variations of this soupy stew, my father's favourite, that you can play around with it endlessly, grabbing whatever is available – instead of chickpeas, use cannellini or haricot beans – and you don't even need the carrots and celery, it's just more interesting with them. If you don't want fish, toast a slice of sourdough, rub it with a halved clove of garlic and drizzle with extra virgin olive oil, then place it in the bottom of your soup bowl.

For 4
1 onion, peeled and chopped
2 garlic cloves, peeled and chopped
2 carrots, peeled and chopped
2 sticks celery, washed and chopped
2 tbsp olive oil
1 bay leaf
1 tsp fresh or ½ tsp dried thyme
1 chorizo (about 100g), sliced
1 x 400g tin chopped tomatoes
1 x 400g tin chickpeas, drained
250ml water
600g cod or pollock fillets, skinned and cut into chunks
salt and pepper

To serve:
extra virgin olive oil

In a large saucepan, soften the onion, garlic, carrots and celery in the olive oil for 5 minutes, stirring every now and again to stop them catching. Add the bay leaf, thyme and sliced chorizo, and heat through until the oil from the chorizo starts to run. Add the tinned tomatoes, drained chickpeas and 250ml water. Bring to the boil, cover with a lid and simmer for 20 minutes, or until the vegetables are soft. Just before the end of cooking, season the fish fillets and add them on top. Replace the lid and cook until done, about 5 minutes, before serving with extra virgin olive oil drizzled over the top.

SUSTAINABLE FISH – A LITTLE RANT

We could all do with eating less meat, right? And maybe less fish, too – though considering a boater's modest plundering of the sea I have largely ignored that one, instead steering you towards a more sustainable catch. So you can do your bit to tackle the depleting fish stocks in our seas and swap your usual cod for a more sustainable variety such as pollock.

According to the experts, if we continue to munch fish at the current rate there will be nothing left by 2048; while discards (the stuff fishermen have to throw back in, dead, if they exceed their quotas) are a continuing issue, which campaigning British chef Hugh Fearnley-Whittingstall is doing his best to fight. You can follow his efforts at www. fishfight.net.

Some of the latest recommendations from the Marine Conservation Society (www.fishonline. org), such as reducing mackerel consumption, have proved controversial, but that's aimed more at the trawlers, not your leisure boater.

For the moment there are plenty more fish in the sea – just not the ones we've been used to eating. So replace haddock and hake with more sustainable gurnard and abundant pouting, instead of salmon opt for trout, in place of sea bass choose sea bream, and rather dogfish than monkfish (forget the name; it tastes great and holds firm in a fish stew). And continue to embrace mussels, sardines, spider crab, pot-caught crab, dabs and flounder. And if you really can't give up your cod, choose sustainably sourced, line-caught, Icelandic cod.

On the tinned tuna front – a permanent fixture in the boat locker – the message about dwindling tuna stocks is finally getting through, and more sustainable skipjack tuna is gaining shelf space –
in the UK, at least. Why does it matter? Because the UK is the biggest consumer of tinned tuna after the USA, so we can have a huge impact on its sustainability.

For more information on the right fish to eat, visit the Marine Stewardship Council at www.msc.org.

Warm spelt salad with leeks, fennel, dill and feta

Spelt is the new grain on the block. It cooks like barley, but it's quicker and has a wonderfully nutty taste. It soaks up flavours well, too, and delivers a satisfying bulk. You can vary the ingredients – instead of fennel, try using broccoli florets or sliced courgettes, boiled just until they still have some bite left. A mix of mushrooms and porcini scattered on top is good, too. In place of dill, use parsley or mint. And if you have a bag of spinach, you can wilt that into the veg at the last minute before combining with the spelt. You can also serve this without the feta as an accompaniment to grilled fish or cold roast chicken.

For 4
2 tbsp olive oil
3 leeks, cut into 5mm slices, rinsed
2 fennel bulbs, rinsed, cut into 5mm slices
200g pearled spelt
handful of dill, finely chopped
juice of 1 lemon
100g feta cheese
extra virgin olive oil
salt and pepper

Heat the olive oil in a large saucepan (I use the pressure cooker pan on board), add the sliced leeks and fennel and a pinch of salt, and put the lid on. Sweat gently over a low heat for 20 minutes until soft, stirring occasionally, adding a splash of water if it starts to stick. Meanwhile, in another saucepan, cook the spelt in salted boiling water for about 20 minutes until just tender – you want a bit of bite – and then drain. Combine with the vegetables, stir in the dill, squeeze the lemon juice over, crumble the feta over and drizzle with a couple of tablespoons of extra virgin olive oil, seasoning as you go.

A lazy guide to filleting a mackerel

Put on a board, belly facing inwards. Lift the fin, put the knife behind it at a 45-degree angle and cut until you hit the spine. Then rotate the knife so that it's flat against the bone.

Pull the knife through the fish, gently skimming the top of the bone. Continue until you've cut through the tail.

Turn the fish over and repeat the process for your second fillet.

Make sure to keep your hand firmly on top of the fish throughout – it will help you control the speed of the knife.

Trim as necessary, removing any dark membrane by gently rubbing with kitchen towel.

Cut either side of the centre line of each fillet at an angle, to create a V shape.

Grab the top of the V section and peel away from the fillet.

To skin, grab the tail end skin side down, and slice into the fish until you hit the skin. Slice away from you until the fillet comes away.

Chilli crab pots

I've always loved crab with chillies, whether it's scoffing a big bowlful of crab linguine specked with them, or diving messily into popular Singapore dish chilli crab. This borrows elements from both, and you can happily use fresh crab instead of tinned – just make sure you have plenty of crusty bread to mop it up.

For 4
3 tbsp olive or rapeseed oil
2 garlic cloves, peeled and crushed
4 tbsp tomato paste
1 tsp mild red chillies, deseeded and chopped
2 x 170g tins white crabmeat chunks in brine, drained
50g Gruyère cheese, grated
black pepper

To serve:
crusty bread
green salad

Preheat the oven to 200°C/fan 180°C/gas 6. Mix the oil, garlic, tomato paste, chillies and crab in a bowl, then season with the pepper. Divide the mixture between four ramekins and top with the cheese. Bake for 10–12 minutes or until the cheese is golden. Serve with crusty bread and a crisp, green salad dressed with vinaigrette (see page 16).

Wave Wisdom
HOW TO KEEP THE SEAGULLS OFF

Decks crusted in guano are one of the most annoying aspects of life at sea, and a lot of time is spent scrubbing them. But sailors have come up with various measures to keep the birds away, from tying carrier bags on pieces of string from the boom – which flutter annoyingly in the wind– to CDs hung from the rigging, flapping and flashing, unsettling gulls (and sailors). And not forgetting the ubiquitous plastic owl, which more often than not acts as a particularly comfy, if rather cocky, perch. Or you could just try scattering a few breadcrumbs on the neighbouring boat (unsporting).

Coconut, chickpea and cauliflower curry

We should all be eating more cauliflower, such are its health benefits. The cauliflower belongs to the cruciferous family, along with broccoli and Brussels sprouts, and contains glucosinolates and thiocyanates, which stimulate the production of cancer-fighting enzymes in the body. Plus it has abundant vitamin C. It delivers on flavour, too, and it's a perfect foil for aromatic spices such as cumin, coriander and turmeric – just what you need after a cold day on the water. Broccoli also works well here.

For 4
300g rice noodles
2 tbsp olive or rapeseed oil
1 onion, peeled and chopped
2 garlic cloves, peeled and chopped
1 tbsp curry powder
1 x 400g tin chickpeas, drained
300g cauliflower florets
1 x 400g tin coconut milk
500ml water

To serve:
handful of fresh coriander, chopped

Cook the noodles as instructed on the packet and drain. Meanwhile, heat the oil in a large pan over a medium heat, add the onion and garlic, and cook for a couple of minutes until soft. Add the curry powder and cook for a minute or so. Add the drained chickpeas and stir to coat. Add the cauliflower, coconut milk and water, then bring to the boil and simmer for 10 minutes, until the cauliflower is tender. To serve, divide the noodles between four deep bowls and top with the curry, then the fresh coriander.

A sort of minestrone

Packed with green vegetables and bolstered by a bit of pasta, this summery soup is a nod to the Italian classic and makes a perfect lunch on the water. You can add whatever green vegetables are available – I like asparagus when it is in season, cut into 2.5cm-long pieces, and green beans also work well. But I particularly love this combination of courgettes, spinach and peas. Orzo, too, is a useful boat staple as it's quick to cook, bolsters soups, and makes a fine salad.

For 4
1 tbsp olive or rapeseed oil
2 shallots or 1 small onion, peeled and finely chopped
1 garlic clove, peeled and crushed
200g new potatoes, cut into small dice
1 courgette, halved and cut into dice
200g young, fresh garden peas
100g orzo pasta (or other soup pasta, such as ditalini)
600ml vegetable or chicken stock
250g ready-washed spinach leaves
salt and pepper

To serve:
Parmesan, grated
handful of basil leaves
olive or rapeseed oil
crusty bread

Heat the oil in a large pan and soften the shallots and garlic for a couple of minutes. Add the potatoes and sauté for another couple of minutes. Then add the courgette, fresh peas, pasta and stock. Cover and cook for 10 minutes. Tip the spinach into the pot, season, replace the lid and cook for another couple of minutes. Serve with a sprinkling of Parmesan, a few torn basil leaves, a drizzle of oil and some crusty bread.

Southern spiced trout fillets with chilli sweetcorn fritters

A winemaker in California first cooked this dish for me using salmon. He was trying to prove that his Pinot Noir went well with fish and stood up to a bit of spice, which it did, rather spectacularly, and I've been cooking this ever since using both salmon and trout. The sweetcorn marries well with the chilli and coriander and brings out the natural sweetness of the fish. Serve with a crisp, green salad.

For 4 – makes 8 fritters
150g plain flour
1 tsp baking powder
125ml milk
2 eggs
1 x 275g tin sweetcorn, drained
4 spring onions, trimmed and chopped
1 tsp red chillies, deseeded and chopped
handful of coriander, chopped
rapeseed oil for frying
3 tsp Spice Mix No. 4 (see page 18)
4 trout fillets
salt and pepper

In a large bowl, combine the flour, a couple of pinches of salt and the baking powder. (You should really sift it, but what's the odd lump when you're on board?) Mix the milk and eggs together, make a well in the flour and add the egg mixture, whisking until smooth. Add the sweetcorn, spring onions, chillies and coriander, and stir until combined. Heat the oil in a frying pan and add 2 tablespoons of batter for each fritter, doing them one at a time if your frying pan is small. Fry for a few minutes until golden on each side, then keep them warm while you cook the trout. Rub the spice mixture on to each side of the fish fillets. Grill the fish for 3–4 minutes on each side until done, season and serve with the warm fritters.

Angela Hartnett's simple fishcakes

You can't have a boat cookbook without fishcakes, and this recipe from Angela Hartnett is about as simple as it gets. Angela is one of the UK's top chefs and the proprietor of London's Michelin-starred Murano restaurant, among others, and she has been awarded an MBE for her efforts. While her cooking at Murano is elegant and refined, at home it's all about comfort food.

For 2
250ml milk
1 garlic clove, peeled and finely sliced
¼ tsp dried thyme
250g pollock fillets, or other white fish fillets
1 floury potato (about 150g), such as King Edward, peeled and cut into 1cm dice
1 tbsp flat-leaf parsley, chopped
1 heaped tbsp flour
3 tbsp olive or rapeseed oil
salt and pepper

To serve:
green salad or wilted spinach

Put the milk, garlic, thyme and fish in a saucepan. Bring to a simmer and cook gently for 3 minutes, then remove from the heat. Lift out the fish from the milk and place in a bowl, then leave to cool a little before flaking with a fork. Add the diced potatoes to the milk and cook for 8 minutes or so until soft. Drain and discard the milk, keeping the garlic, thyme and potatoes. Add the potatoes and garlic to the flaked fish, along with the parsley, then mash with a fork until everything is combined and season well. Divide the mixture into four and mould with your hands into rounds. Allow to cool (ideally chill for 20 minutes) before sprinkling flour over both sides and shallow frying in oil until golden on both sides and warmed through. Serve with a green salad or some wilted spinach.

Salad of shaved fennel, frisée, Parmesan and toasted almonds with prosciutto

This simple salad is a satisfying balance of textures and salty, toasty flavours. And if you take away the prosciutto, you have a perfect accompaniment to grilled fish or meat.

For 4
100g whole blanched almonds
1 fennel bulb, rinsed and trimmed
1 frisée lettuce, washed and torn
50g Parmesan
8 slices of prosciutto (or other air-dried ham)

For the dressing:
3 tbsp olive or rapeseed oil
1 tbsp white wine vinegar
salt and pepper

Toast the almonds in a frying pan for a few minutes until lightly browned, then cool. Using either a wide-bladed vegetable peeler or a mandolin, shave the fennel paper-thin into a mixing bowl. Add the toasted almonds and torn lettuce and, with the same peeler, shave the Parmesan over. Mix the dressing ingredients together and combine with the salad. Serve with the slices of prosciutto.

Crab macaroni cheese

Macaroni cheese is my ultimate boat comfort food – add crab and it becomes something special. A fresh, dressed crab is the best thing to use here, as it cranks up the flavour intensity, but you can use a tub of pasteurised white crabmeat, or failing that two 170g tins of white crabmeat. Serve with a crisp, green salad.

For 4
50g butter
2 leeks, trimmed, washed and finely sliced
400g macaroni, or other short pasta
50g flour
600ml milk
150g mature Cheddar, grated
¼ tsp nutmeg, grated
1 dressed crab
2 handfuls of breadcrumbs
salt and pepper

Melt the butter in a heavy-bottomed pan and add the leeks, then cover and sweat for 10 minutes to soften. Meanwhile bring salted water to the boil in a large saucepan and cook the pasta, then drain and keep warm. Heat the grill. Add the flour to the leeks, stir to combine and cook for a couple of minutes. Gradually add the milk, whisking to avoid lumps, and simmer for 5 minutes. Add half the cheese and all of the nutmeg and crab, then heat through and season before stirring in the cooked pasta. Tip the lot into a shallow baking dish if you are using a boat grill (if you are cooking at home with a larger grill, any heatproof dish will work). Top with the breadcrumbs and the remaining cheese. Grill for a couple of minutes until the topping is crunchy and golden.

～Wave Wisdom
THE ART OF CRABBING

Actually, there is no art to crabbing – in fact, you'll rarely come back empty-handed. All you need is a long-handled net, a bucket, a line and some bait. Blag a few fish heads from a local fisherman, or better, save any chicken scraps from supper (caviar for crabs) and grab a pitch – piers and pontoons are always good; a steady stream of local children usually bag the best spots, so follow the scramble of buckets and nets. There aren't any essential techniques, just ninja reflexes when it comes to scooping them up in your net. And watch the pincers – consider investing in a pair of thick leather gloves.

Grilled lemony chicken breasts with olive, red pepper and pine nut couscous

A good one for the barbecue. Served with this clever little locker salad, it makes the perfect boat food. Prepare the chicken a few hours earlier if you prefer – it will happily sit in its marinade in a ziplock plastic bag in the coolbox until you are ready to cook.

For 4

1 tbsp dried oregano
1 tsp chilli flakes
4 tbsp olive or rapeseed oil
juice of 2 lemons, plus the grated zest of 1
4 large free-range chicken breasts
salt and lots of black pepper

For the couscous:
250g couscous
400ml boiling water
1 tbsp olive or rapeseed oil
1 x 280g jar roasted red peppers in olive oil, drained, reserving 1 tbsp oil, and cut into strips
100g pine nuts, toasted
150g pitted olives
handful of coriander or flat-leaf parsley, chopped
salt and pepper

Combine the oregano, chilli flakes, oil and lemon zest in a ziplock bag and shove in the chicken, making sure everything gets covered in the marinade. Leave for 30 minutes. Meanwhile, put the couscous in a bowl and add the boiling water and oil. Cover with clingfilm, then leave to swell for 5 minutes. Once all the water has been absorbed, stir in the sliced roasted red peppers with the reserved pepper oil, toasted pine nuts, olives and chopped herbs. Season.

When you are ready to cook the chicken, squeeze the juice of one of the lemons over it and grill for about 5 minutes on each side, until done. Remove from the heat. Squeeze the juice from the remaining lemon over and leave to rest for 5–10 minutes before saesoning and serving with the couscous.

Ria's smoked mackerel kedgeree with spring onions and crème fraîche

Kedgeree is one of my all-time favourite brunch dishes, and this recipe is up there with the best of them. First served to me by keen home cook and Isle of Wight resident Ria King, it uses smoked mackerel instead of the more traditional haddock, which adds a satisfying richness cut through by the crème fraîche and the crunch of spring onions. Ria's husband, Mark, smokes the fish himself (see page 120 if you want to try this yourself), and when he's not catching fish, he's playing in his legendary soul funk band, Level 42.

For 4

25g butter

1 onion, peeled and finely chopped

1 fat clove of garlic, peeled and crushed

2 tsp mild curry powder

300g basmati rice

1 litre fish stock or vegetable bouillon

4 eggs

350g smoked mackerel fillets, skinned and flaked

2 tbsp crème fraîche

4 spring onions, trimmed and chopped

handful of flat-leaf parsley, chopped

Melt the butter, then add the chopped onion and fry gently for a few minutes until soft. Add the garlic and curry powder, and then the rice, giving it all a good stir. Add the stock and simmer for 12 minutes or so, stirring frequently. Meanwhile, boil the eggs for 7 minutes, shell and cut into quarters. Add the mackerel, crème fraîche, spring onions and half the parsley to the rice, and heat through for another couple of minutes. Spoon into bowls, place the egg quarters on top and sprinkle with the remaining chopped parsley.

DIGGING FOR BAIT

You want to catch some fish? You'll need some decent bait, then. On the Isle of Wight, that means knocking on Barney Coupland's front door. Barney's Bait is an island institution, and Barney operates the business from his sitting room in Cowes, seven days a week. In fact, it was Barney's bait that hooked a record stingray from nearby Thorness Bay – his kitchen is covered with photos of the fish his customers have caught with his bait. 'You need to know where your bait comes from. And it's all about freshness and size – like a good steak,' explains Barney. He has 20 different kinds of bait in stock at any one time, from ragworm to sand eels, and has regular customers from Portsmouth to Southampton. 'Without good bait you aren't going anywhere,' he says. Every fishing hub will have a Barney, so quiz local fishermen before seeking them out.

Sardines on toast with pine nuts and capers

Not a week goes by without me opening a can of sardines to tip on to toast. Sometimes I eat them as they come; other times I dress them up like this.

For 4

4 thick slices of sourdough bread
1 garlic clove, halved
drizzle of olive or rapeseed oil
4 x 100g tins sardine fillets, drained
1 lemon
handful of flat-leaf parsley, chopped
2 tbsp pine nuts, lightly toasted
1 tbsp salted capers, rinsed
1 tbsp red onion, finely chopped
salt and pepper

Preheat the grill to medium-high. Line the grill pan with foil and toast the bread on each side. Rub the toasted bread on one side with the halved garlic clove. Drizzle with a little oil. Flake the sardines over the toast. Finally, zest the lemon. Combine the parsley, pine nuts, capers, onion and lemon zest in a small bowl, season and mix well. Sprinkle evenly over the sardines, and serve with the quartered lemon.

Ceviche

I've been a bit obsessed with this Peruvian dish ever since I travelled to Lima to write an article about the country's cuisine. As the sun rose over the fishing harbour at Chorillos, we watched chefs barter for the best fish, then joined them for a breakfast of the national dish prepared by harbourside vendors, who combined the daily catch (sole is the most highly prized fish for ceviche) with limes, chillies and onions. And yes, there is a fair bit of salt in the marinade – it's essential for 'cooking' the raw fish, but you do drain most of it off. It's the new sushi, but easier to make. A fine light lunch or starter.

For 4

1 small red onion, peeled and very thinly sliced
4 limes
handful of coriander, chopped
2cm piece of ginger, peeled and finely grated
1 garlic clove, peeled and crushed
600g skinless lemon sole fillets (or sea bream)
1 medium red chilli, deseeded and finely chopped
1 tsp Maldon salt

Wash the red onion, leave to soak in cold water for 10 minutes to tone down its strength, then drain. Meanwhile, roll each lime on a table to warm up and loosen the juice, then squeeze into a bowl. Add half the chopped coriander, along with the ginger and garlic. Cut the fish into 1–2cm pieces. Sprinkle the salt over the fish, then add it to the bowl, gently turning in the juice to ensure it is properly covered. Set aside for 10 minutes to let the fish 'cook' in the marinade. When you are ready to serve, mix with the onions, chillies and remaining coriander and serve immediately.

Barbecued herb-stuffed trout

I'm going to bang the drum for farmed trout. Our supermarkets are groaning with farmed salmon, but trout only gets a fraction of the shelf space. It tastes just as delicious and it's sustainable, so what's not to like? If you are catching your own fish, then this marinade works for pretty much every decent-sized whole fish, including mackerel. You just need to gut the fish, descale if necessary, and you are ready to go. Little tip: use a fish grilling rack so you can turn it without it falling apart.

For 4
4 whole farmed trout, gutted, rinsed and patted dry

For the marinade:
grated zest and juice of 2 lemons
1 tbsp fresh thyme, chopped (or 1 tsp if you are using dried thyme)
1 handful of flat-leaf parsley, roughly chopped
1 handful of fresh mint, roughly chopped
75ml olive or rapeseed oil
salt and pepper
extra olive or rapeseed oil

To serve:
1 lemon, quartered
couple of handfuls of samphire (optional)

Combine the ingredients for the marinade. Set aside half for the dressing. Divide the rest of the marinade between each trout, placing it in the cavity. Rub the outside of the fish with oil. Brush the fish grill with a little more oil to prevent sticking. Place the fish in the grill rack and cook for 7 minutes on one side, then flip and cook until the fish is opaque in the centre (about 7 minutes more). Serve with the remaining herb marinade, the lemon quarters and samphire, if you can find some, cooked as below.

SEXY SAMPHIRE

Once something the fishmonger slipped in with your purchase as an afterthought, samphire is now on the menu in top restaurants around the country. Also known as glasswort, it is a succulent plant that grows around estuaries and tidal creeks and has a satisfying crunch and salty tang. You can gather it yourself when in season from June to September. There are two types: marsh and rock samphire, and it looks a bit like a small cactus minus the spines – just pinch off the juicy tops (or buy at the supermarket). To cook, rinse and rinse again, then boil in salted water for 3–4 minutes before draining, tossing with butter or olive oil, and serving with a squeeze of lemon and some crisp-skinned grilled mackerel.

Brown shrimps with borlotti beans and cherry tomatoes

These little beauties pack a punch in the flavour department. The best are the tiny, sweet crustaceans found on the tidal sands of Morecambe Bay and along the north Norfolk coast, and are a classic ingredient in potted shrimps. But North Sea brown shrimps are almost as good and easy to find at the fishmonger or in certain supermarkets, cooked, minus their shells, in 90g packs; or you can, of course, replace them with regular Atlantic cooked prawns. The different hues of pink in this salad look rather fetching, too.

For 4

180g cooked and shelled brown shrimps

1 x 400g tin borlotti beans, rinsed and drained

250g cherry tomatoes, halved

1 shallot, peeled and finely chopped, or 3 spring onions, trimmed and sliced

handful of flat-leaf parsley, chopped

2 tbsp extra virgin olive oil

juice of 1 lemon

salt and pepper

In a bowl, combine the shrimps, beans, tomatoes, shallots and parsley. Drizzle with the oil, squeeze the lemon over and season. Serve piled on to toasted sourdough, or as a salad with some ready-washed leaves stirred through.

Mike Golding's chilli beef noodles with broccoli and cashew nuts ☼

One of the world's most accomplished offshore sailors, former firefighter Mike Golding has notched up over 250,000 sailing miles (including five spins around Cape Horn) and accumulated several world records, gaining an OBE for his efforts. At sea it's all about freeze-dried food, as for every competing sailor, but in harbour he's more adventurous. Mike's boat tucker of choice? Strips of beef, stir-fried with ginger and chillies.

For 2

2 tbsp rapeseed oil

300g thin-cut beef sirloin, cut into strips

2 garlic cloves, peeled and finely sliced

5cm piece of ginger, peeled and finely chopped

1 tsp dried chillies, crushed, or 1 fresh red chilli, de-seeded and sliced

2 tbsp light soy sauce

juice of 1 lime

1 tsp sugar

250g egg noodles

200g tenderstem broccoli

4 spring onions, trimmed and sliced

50g unsalted cashew nuts, or rinsed salted cashews, chopped

Heat 1 tablespoon of the oil and stir-fry the beef, garlic, ginger and chillies until almost cooked. Add the soy sauce, lime juice and sugar and cook for another minute. Tip into a bowl and set aside. Prepare the egg noodles according to the instructions on the packet and drain. Put the pan back on the heat and add the remaining oil, the broccoli and spring onions and stir-fry for a couple of minutes. Return the beef mixture to the pan to heat through, then stir in the cashew nuts and the noodles. Divvy up.

Roasted peaches with honey and pecans

The simplest desserts are often the most elegant, and you can't argue with this classic combo. Nectarines also work well in this recipe. Makes a rather fine breakfast, too.

For 4

4 peaches or nectarines (unpeeled), halved and stones removed
100ml orange juice
4 knobs of butter
2 tbsp runny honey
50g pecan nuts, roughly chopped

To serve:
Greek yoghurt or crème fraîche

Preheat the oven to 200°C/fan 180°C/gas 6. Place the peaches or nectarines cut side up on a baking tray, pour the orange juice over, put a knob of butter in the centre of each fruit, drizzle with the honey and scatter with the nuts. Roast for 10–15 minutes, depending on their ripeness. Serve with the juices and some Greek yoghurt or crème fraîche.

Cheat's plum, cinnamon and ginger crumble

Not a complete cheat as you've got to cook the plums. The nation's favourite pud, the classic British crumble has been tweaked and tarted up in homes and restaurants across the country. This one is about as minimalist as it gets, but the texture and flavour are all there – and ginger is a hit with plums.

2 tbsp sugar
8 large ripe plums, halved and stoned
25g butter
1 tsp ground cinnamon
6 gingernut biscuits

To serve:
crème fraîche or ready-made custard

Preheat the oven to 200°C/fan 180°C/gas 6. Mix the sugar with a couple of tablespoons of water in an ovenproof dish. Add the plums cut side up, dot with butter in the hollow and sprinkle with the cinnamon. Bake for 10 minutes or until the plums are tender (depends how ripe your fruit is). Place the gingernuts in a plastic bag and crush with a wine bottle, or equivalent. Spoon the crumbs over the plums and return to the oven for a few more minutes to let them brown a little. Serve with crème fraîche or custard.

Kevin Mangeolles' prune (or cherry) clafoutis 👨‍🍳

I've taken to the water a few times with Michelin-starred chef Kevin Mangeolles. He used to head up the kitchen at The George in Yarmouth, and then he upped sticks to another beautiful part of the British coast, north Norfolk, where he continues to do innovative things at The Neptune Inn and Restaurant in Old Hunstanton. Kevin's cooking is classically based with a fresh, modern approach – a bit like his clafoutis recipe, which he has kindly shared. I sometimes leave the stones in, as they do in Limousin, where this fruit batter pudding originates, but on the boat I prefer to prise them out. If you can't find fresh cherries, tinned ones work, too.

For 4
1 egg plus 2 egg yolks
3 tbsp caster sugar
3 tbsp plain flour
150ml double cream
1 x 420g tin of prunes, drained (or 200g fresh cherries)

To serve:
double cream or creme fraiche (optional)

Preheat the oven to 200°C/fan 180°C/gas 6 and grease a 20cm ovenproof dish. Beat the eggs with the sugar, then fold in the flour followed by the double cream. Scrape into the greased dish then arrange the prunes in the batter. Bake for 15 minutes until set and golden. Serve warm, on its own or with cream or crème fraîche.

Oranges with pistachios and mascarpone

This is so refreshing, and just a little bit wicked thanks to the mascarpone. And it's especially good after a rich stew. You can replace the mascarpone and low-fat yoghurt combo with Greek yoghurt, if you prefer. Good served with cranberry, orange and pumpkin seed flapjacks (see page 133).

For 4
2 oranges
2 tbsp orange marmalade
125g mascarpone
125g low-fat yoghurt
50g pistachios, shelled and chopped

Cut off the rind and pith from the oranges and segment them, keeping any juice that runs free. Combine the juice with the marmalade and add the segments, stirring to combine. Mix the mascarpone and yoghurt and divide between 4 glasses. Top with the orange mixture and pistachios, and serve.

TEN GREAT UK HARBOUR TOWNS

POOLE, DORSET
A large, natural harbour once favoured by the Romans, Poole is surrounded by miles of golden sandy beaches.

CHICHESTER, HAMPSHIRE
South-west of the city of Chichester on the Solent, the popular harbour remains surprisingly wild, with its warren of creeks a haven for wildlife.

TOBERMORY, ISLE OF MULL
Located in the Scottish Inner Hebrides, the achingly pretty harbour, with its brightly coloured houses, is a film producer's dream.

DARTMOUTH, DEVON
The Crusades once sailed from this town at the mouth of the River Dart estuary and it was once home to the Royal Navy. Don't miss the annual regatta, held in August.

FOWEY, CORNWALL
Dating back to the Domesday Book, the picturesque town tumbles down the hillside to the quaint waterfront. Smuggling here was once de rigueur.

YARMOUTH, ISLE OF WIGHT
The prettiest place on the Isle of Wight, located to the west of the island; it boasts a largely Georgian town square and the longest timber pier in England.

BURNHAM-ON-CROUCH, ESSEX
On the north bank of the River Crouch, Burnham has seen yachting replace oysters as the main draw, with its annual regatta, Burnham Week, taking place in August.

ST PETER PORT, GUERNSEY
The capital of Guernsey, it's a small, atmospheric town of narrow streets and steep steps, located on the island's east coast.

PORT ST MARY, ISLE OF MAN
It takes its name from the former chapel of St Mary on the south-western side of the island. Don't miss the steam train, which runs all the way to Douglas.

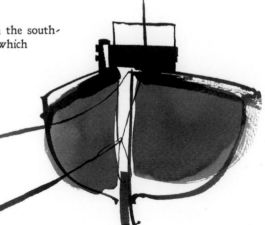

DONAGHADEE, COUNTY DOWN
Complete with a moat and lighthouse, the town is situated on the Ards Peninsula on the Irish Sea coast. On a clear day you can see Scotland.

At Sea

When the waves are up and the wind is whipping the halyards, setting foot below deck for more than a few minutes can be tricky, especially when it comes to fiddling around with food. So the following recipes are simpler, more sustaining, and use ingredients stowed within easy reach. Tins are more the focus here, but fresh ingredients are incorporated with abundance, particularly when it comes to herbs.

I haven't compromised on fresh herbs in this book. I figure that, like me, the average boater is at sea only for a few days, tucking into harbours or dropping anchor in a quiet bay or marina for lunch and at the end of each day. And fresh herbs, indeed most other fresh ingredients, will sit quite happily in the cool box for a couple of days without any ill effect. Fresh herbs will transform a dish in a way that dried herbs never could (spaghetti with tuna, olives, capers, tomatoes and basil is a case in point, see page 90), so it's worth bringing them along.

Everything tastes better on the water. There's no scientific proof, of course; it just seems to be that way. Even the dodgiest of concoctions – I'm thinking specifically of my dad's boat beef curry lunch (cheapest supermarket tinned beef stew laced with a couple of teaspoons of hot curry powder). It wouldn't normally get past my lips, but after a long sail it tastes pretty good.

We rarely cook on the move, but wait until we are at anchor in some bay or river, like most of you, I suspect. And even if you did need to rustle something up in transit, you probably wouldn't set foot in the galley beyond a Force 4 for more than a couple of minutes. Still, with changeable weather the most frequent forecast in the British Isles, it pays to think ahead and prepare as much as you can in advance: drain tins, chop vegetables, combine spices, and so on.

Baked eggs with hot-smoked salmon and dill

Eggs and smoked salmon for breakfast are up there with the Full English. This is just a twist on the classic, and even quicker to prepare. You could smoke your own fish at home or on the beach (see page 120). I also make this with smoked mackerel – a stronger flavour, sure, but it works well with the eggs, cream and dill. Make sure you have some toast slathered with butter at the ready.

For 4
1 tbsp butter
200g hot-smoked salmon, flaked
4 large free-range eggs
4 tbsp crème fraîche
1 tbsp dill, chopped
salt and pepper

Preheat the oven to 200°C/fan 180°C/gas 6. Grease four metal ramekins with some of the butter and divide the fish between them. Break an egg into each one, season, then divvy up the crème fraîche, finishing with the dill and a small knob of butter on top of each dish. Place on a baking tray and cook for 8–12 minutes until the whites are set and the yolk is still a bit soft.

Cheese, ham and mushroom quesadillas

These are addictive, you have been warned – all that crisp tortilla and oozing melted cheese. It's Mexico's answer to the toasted cheese sandwich. You can play around with the fillings, too: try sliced salami or chorizo, or add chopped red chilli for a spicy kick, and sliced tomatoes. And if you can't get Emmental, any mild, hard cheese will do.

For 2
4 wholemeal flour tortillas
2 fistfuls of ready-grated Emmental
2 slices of air-dried, roasted or boiled ham
40g mushrooms, thinly sliced

You'll have to make these in two batches. Heat a non-stick frying pan until hot and slide in the first tortilla. Scatter a quarter of the cheese over and cover with a slice of ham and half the mushrooms, then top with another quarter of cheese and a second tortilla. In a couple of minutes have a peek and, if it's looking nicely browned, flip it over carefully with a fish slice. Cook on the other side, pressing down gently with the slice to compact the quesadilla. Once brown on both sides, slide it on to a chopping board, cut into wedges and start munching. Then start all over again with the second tortilla.

THE SHIPPING FORECAST DEMYSTIFIED

The shipping forecast is part of our heritage, as British as the chimes of Big Ben. As well as guiding boats safely around our shores and away from our sandbanks, its slow methodical delivery has become an unintentional relaxation aid for landlubbers, who tune in for its broadcasts in the early hours to listen to the poetic place names, even if most don't know where they are – Viking and Forties, Humber and Bailey.

Every single word of the 11-minute forecast has its own specific meaning; even general words have a precise reference. The word 'then' takes on surprising importance – if an area has two types of weather, it is the most severe one that takes precedence, for example, 'rain, then showers'; if a wind is 'veering' it's changing direction on a clockwise route; if it's 'backing' it's doing the opposite. A soothing presence to fishermen braving big seas, the shipping forecast also works its lullaby magic on those of us tucked up safely in bed.

Fried bananas on toast with walnuts and maple syrup

I love banana pancakes and I love French toast, so why not bananas on toast? This thought came to me one chilly morning when in need of a sugar hit to start the day, and it now makes a regular appearance at the breakfast table, boat or home. If you can find a brioche loaf, then cut it into thick slices before toasting, but really any crusty white loaf will do. There's enough sweetness in the bananas and maple syrup to keep everyone happy.

For 2
2 bananas
25g butter
juice of ½ lemon or lime
25g walnuts or pecans, roughly chopped
2 thick slices of crusty white bread
2 tbsp maple syrup
salt and pepper

Slice the bananas lengthways. Melt the butter in a frying pan and slide in the bananas, squeezing the lemon or lime juice over them. Cook until soft and slightly golden on both sides, then transfer to a plate. Add the nuts to the pan and lightly brown. Meanwhile, toast the bread. Load the banana mixture on to the bread, followed by the nuts, and drizzle the maple syrup over.

Red flannel hash

This is my version of an old New England breakfast dish that gets its name from the colour of a colonial plaid cloth. It's basically corned beef hash with beetroot in it. It's not a combination you would immediately think of, but it works, and rather spectacularly. And I know how much sailors (my dad particularly) are attached to their tins of corned beef.

For 4

3 tbsp olive or rapeseed oil
500g waxy potatoes, peeled and diced
1 onion, peeled and chopped
1 x 340g tin corned beef, diced
250g cooked beetroot, in natural juice, drained and diced
4 large free-range eggs
salt and pepper

Heat the oil in a sauté pan, add the potatoes and turn every now and again until almost cooked through. Add the onion and cook for another 2–3 minutes, until translucent. Add the corned beef and the beetroot, season and heat through for a couple of minutes. Make four indentations and break the eggs into them. Cover the pan and let the eggs poach in the mixture: 5 minutes for runny yolks, 7 minutes for firm yolks. Serve immediately.

Eggs with coriander, chilli and yoghurt

There's nothing like a bit of chilli to wake up the palate on a frosty morning, and this Turkish-inspired egg, coriander and yoghurt combo has proved to be a big hit – all your breakfast needs on one zingy plate. Best scooped up with a hunk of crusty bread.

For 2

1 garlic clove, peeled and crushed
200g Greek yoghurt
4 medium free-range eggs
1 tsp mild red chilli, deseeded and chopped
2 tbsp coriander, chopped
salt

Preheat the grill to high. Crush the garlic into the salt and mix with the yoghurt. Crack the eggs into a small frying pan, then dollop the yoghurt mixture over the eggs. Season with salt and sprinkle with the chilli and coriander. Place under the grill and cook for about 5 minutes or until the whites are firm and the yolks are slightly runny.

SEASICKNESS REMEDIES

There are three guaranteed triggers for seasickness: going below for any length of time, looking through binoculars for anything longer than a glance, and trying to read a book. There are over-the-counter and prescription drugs, plus homeopathic remedies galore, not to mention pressure point wristbands, which seem to be effective in my very unscientific trials. For me, ginger is a good natural alternative. Nibble on shop-bought candied ginger, or make your own by slicing the peeled root thinly, covering with honey and letting it stand for a couple of weeks before draining and patting dry. Or make a tea with ground ginger, adding 1 teaspoon to a mug of boiling water and letting it steep for a few minutes, adding honey to taste. Though do check with your doc before consuming as it may interfere with other drugs.

Penne with sardines, saffron and pine nuts

Or pasta con sarde, as they call it in Sicily. Instead of fiddling around with fresh sardines, tinned fish works really well here. The combination of salt and sweet layered with nuts and laced with saffron is moreish, and I can't get enough of it.

For 4

2 tbsp olive or rapeseed oil

1 small onion, peeled and chopped

50g tin anchovies, drained and chopped

1 tbsp sultanas

1 tsp fennel seeds

2 tbsp pine nuts

300ml water

1 tbsp tomato paste

pinch of saffron

2 x 120g tins sardine fillets in olive oil, drained

400g penne pasta

1 slice of bread, crusts removed, grated to make breadcrumbs

Bring a pan of salted water to the boil for the pasta. Heat the oil in another pan and soften the onion for 5 minutes. Add the anchovies and heat through until mostly 'melted', stirring regularly. Add the sultanas, fennel seeds and pine nuts, and cook for a couple of minutes. Add the water, tomato paste and saffron, and cook for 8 minutes. Add the sardines, breaking them up a bit, and heat through. Meanwhile, cook the pasta until al dente. Add the pasta to the sauce and stir in the grated bread. Let it sit for a couple of minutes for the flavours to mingle before serving.

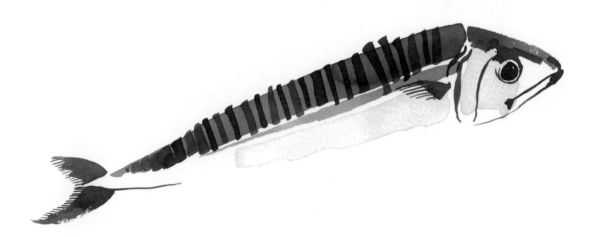

Brian Thompson's sautéed squid with parsley, lemon and garlic mayonnaise ☸

Brian Thompson has more multihull sailing miles under his belt than any other Brit, and has notched up an impressive 25 sailing records, including fastest around-the-world non-stop speed sailing. Most of the food Brian cooks on board is freeze-dried, granted, but every now and again he is rewarded with squid that he finds on deck (yes, squid fly), which he'll fry up with some garlic. Once back on land, he'll add freshly chopped parsley and a squeeze of lemon before dipping into mayonnaise. Try serving it over some crunchy romaine lettuce.

For 2 (or 4, as a starter)
2 garlic cloves, peeled and crushed
few dollops of good mayonnaise
450g small squid, cleaned
1 tbsp olive or rapeseed oil
1 tbsp unsalted butter
handful of flat-leaf parsley, chopped
1 lemon, cut into wedges
1 tsp chopped chilli (optional)
salt and pepper

Stir one of the crushed garlic cloves into the mayonnaise. Pull off the little tentacles from the squid, pat dry with a paper towel and set aside. Cut the squid into 2cm rings. Heat the oil in a deep saucepan until smoking. Add the squid rings and tentacles in a single layer, then add the butter, the other crushed garlic clove and the parsley. Cook, tossing frequently, for 1–2 minutes until the squid is opaque and cooked through. Season and serve with the lemon wedges and the garlic mayonnaise.

Judy Joo's cowboy laksa

I'm using kitchen slang here – cowboy laksa is just lazy laksa, a nod to the famous South East Asian aromatic noodle soup, best found on a street corner in Singapore. I was first served this dish by chef and TV presenter Judy Joo, who continually plunders her Korean (via New York) heritage for addictive spicy noodle recipes, and this one has become a firm favourite on board – it's quick, packs a punch, and will make you smile. You can use cooked peeled prawns instead of chicken, adding them in at the end to heat through.

For 4
250g rice vermicelli noodles
1 tbsp olive or rapeseed oil
4 tbsp laksa paste
200ml coconut milk
600ml chicken stock (or water)
600g chicken breast, sliced thinly

Optional:
2 handfuls of pak choi leaves, or spinach
2 handfuls of bean sprouts
handful of coriander, chopped

Place the noodles in a bowl, cover with boiling water and leave to soften for about 5 minutes before rinsing with cold water, draining and dividing between 4 deep soup bowls. Heat the oil in a large saucepan and sauté the laksa paste for a minute. Add the coconut milk and stock or water and bring up to a simmer, mixing well to dissolve the paste (I use a whisk). Add the chicken and simmer for 5 minutes until cooked through, then add the bean sprouts and pak choi or spinach, if you are using it, and cook for another couple of minutes. Spoon over the noodles and serve, garnished with the chopped coriander if you have some.

FIVE OF THE BEST UK SAILING EVENTS

WEST HIGHLAND YACHTING WEEK

Now in its 65th year, this is the west coast of Scotland's second biggest sailing event, taking in three venues: Craobh, Oban and Tobermory. Set against jaw-dropping scenery, it sees over 1,000 competitors from all around the world combine racing with social events.

www.whyw.co.uk

ROUND THE ISLAND

The historic race around the Isle of Wight celebrated its 80th anniversary in 2011. First started by the Island Sailing Club for smaller boats, it is now an important part of the competition calendar for all boats, which cross the line at Cowes in 11 separate groups, starting every 10 minutes from 05.00 until 06.40 in a westerly direction towards Yarmouth – quite a spectacle.

www.roundtheisland.org.uk

COWES WEEK

The granddaddy of British sailing events, Cowes Week is one of the UK's longest-running sporting occasions, held every August since 1826 (except during the two world wars). Awash with royalty and celebs, it now sees over 1,000 boats in up to 40 different handicaps, one-design and multihull classes racing every day for eight days.

www.lendycowesweek.co.uk

DARTMOUTH ROYAL REGATTA

The first regatta was held on the River Dart back in 1822 and it's been going strong ever since, thanks in part to royal patronage – today in the person of HRH the Duke of York – but also because of the legion of local volunteers who make it happen. It's held over three days on the last weekend in August and is based around a programme of rowing and sailing events.

www.dartmouthregatta.co.uk

BURNHAM WEEK

With a history that dates back to 1893, Burnham Week is the last event of the year in the sailing regatta calendar, but by no means the least. Taking place in the Essex harbour town of Burnham-on-Crouch, it attracts boats large and small, which compete for the impressive Town Cup. Past winners include the then British Prime Minister, the Right Hon. Edward Heath MP, in *Morning Cloud*.

www.burnhamweek.org.uk

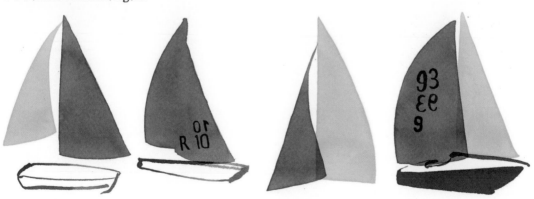

Orecchiette with broccoli, walnuts, sun-dried tomatoes and basil

I'm always on the lookout for punchy meat-free pasta sauces and this one scores highly, from the superfood status granted to broccoli and walnuts, to the flavour bomb in the form of sun-dried tomatoes and heady, galley-scenting basil.

For 4

2 tbsp walnuts, roughly chopped
1 tbsp olive or rapeseed oil
2 garlic cloves, peeled and finely chopped
2 tbsp sun-dried tomatoes, roughly chopped
2 heads of broccoli, chopped into small florets
500g orecchiette or penne pasta
salt and black pepper

To serve:
Parmesan cheese, freshly grated

Heat a small saucepan and add the walnuts, stirring as you lightly toast them. Remove the walnuts and wipe the pan clean carefully with kitchen towel. Once it's cooled off a bit put the pan back on the heat and add the olive oil and garlic, letting the garlic lightly brown, then turn it off and add the sun-dried tomatoes and toasted walnuts.

Fill a larger saucepan with water and bring to the boil, add the broccoli and let it cook until very tender. Remove the broccoli with a slotted spoon and add to the smaller pan with the garlic, walnuts and sun-dried tomatoes, smashing the broccoli down with a wooden spoon. Season.

Add the pasta to the broccoli water and cook until al dente, then drain and stir into the broccoli sauce. Serve with grated Parmesan cheese.

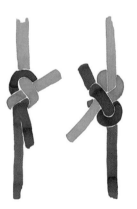

SPLICE THE MAIN BRACE

The great sailing ships were propelled only by the wind in their sails, which were attached to spars called yards. The lines to trim the sails were called braces, and ran from the end of the yards to the deck. The main brace was the largest and heaviest of the rigging, and to splice it was one of the most difficult jobs. But those that put in the effort to 'splice the main brace' got a double issue of rum. Result.

Tuna, cannellini bean and marinated artichoke salad

All you need is a handful of parsley and a small red onion and the rest is straight from the locker. This simple, punchy, sustaining salad makes a regular appearance for lunch when we're at sea and is a good one to rustle up when you have unexpected company. You can play around with the ingredients, too – add a few sun-dried tomatoes, and stir in a bag of rocket or watercress.

For 4

1 x 200g tin tuna, drained

1 x 280g jar marinated artichoke hearts in olive oil, drained

1 x 400g tin cannellini beans, drained and rinsed

1 small red onion, peeled and chopped

handful of flat-leaf parsley, chopped

extra virgin olive or rapeseed oil, to drizzle

salt and black pepper

Flake the tuna into a bowl. Add the artichokes, beans, onion and parsley and combine. Season, and serve with a generous drizzle of olive oil.

Fish stew with gremolata

There are dozens of fish stew recipes, some created with such reverence and painstaking labour that they take a whole day to make, but the best are often the simplest, and this one offers maximum flavour with minimum effort. It pays homage to that Maltese staple, aljotta, and it's lifted with an Italian-style zesty gremolata. And as in a classic aljotta, you can use whatever fish is available.

For 4

2 tbsp olive or rapeseed oil
1 small onion, peeled and finely chopped
2 garlic cloves, peeled and crushed
pinch of saffron, soaked in 1 tbsp boiling water
½ tsp smoked paprika
1 tbsp fresh mint, chopped
1 tbsp tomato paste
500ml fish or vegetable stock
300ml dry white wine (red wine works, too)
100g long grain rice
1 x 400g tin chopped tomatoes
400g skinless firm fish fillets (try cod or pollock), cut into 3–4cm pieces
salt and pepper

For the gremolata:
grated zest of 1 lemon
handful of flat-leaf parsley, finely chopped
1 garlic clove, peeled and crushed

Heat the oil in a large pan and soften the onion and garlic. Add the saffron and its soaking water, and the paprika, mint and tomato paste. Cook for a minute, then add the stock, wine, rice and tomatoes. Bring to the boil and simmer for 10 minutes, stirring every now and again to stop the rice sticking on the bottom. Season, then add the fish, cover and cook for 5 more minutes, or until the fish is cooked. Meanwhile, make the gremolata by mixing the lemon, parsley and garlic. Serve the stew with the gremolata spooned over the top.

Spaghetti with tuna, olives, capers, tomatoes and basil

This has been one of my boat staples since I first started cooking on board. Capers and olives have an affinity with tuna and when combined they do a little jig in the mouth. Another good one for unexpected guests.

For 4

2 tbsp olive or rapeseed oil
1 medium onion, peeled and chopped
1 garlic clove, peeled and crushed
4 sun-dried tomatoes, chopped
1 tbsp green or black olives, pitted and finely chopped
1 tbsp capers, rinsed
1 x 400g tin chopped tomatoes
100ml dry white wine
500g spaghetti
1 x 200g tin tuna, drained
8 basil leaves, torn, or 1 tbsp flat-leaf parsley, chopped
salt and pepper

Heat the oil in a saucepan. Add the chopped onion and soften for 5 minutes. Add the garlic, sun-dried tomatoes, olives and capers and cook for another couple of minutes. Add the tinned tomatoes and the wine, and simmer uncovered for 10 minutes or so until the mixture has thickened. Meanwhile, bring salted water to the boil in another saucepan and cook the spaghetti until al dente. Add the drained tuna and the basil or parsley to the sauce, season, stir in the cooked spaghetti, and serve.

GREAT BOATING NOVELS

When the weather closes in, it's time to anchor up and hunker down with a good book – so make it one with a nautical theme, such as a great seafaring tale like *Moby Dick* by Herman Melville. Melville's anarchic, eccentric masterpiece tells the story of Captain Ahab and his obsessive quest for a whale, whose terrifying whiteness comes to embody evil itself. Or scare yourself silly with *The Perfect Storm* by Sebastian Junger, which sees three weather systems collide off the coast of Nova Scotia to create the mother of all storms, complete with hundred-foot waves. Or learn how not to captain a ship in *The Caine Mutiny* by Herman Wouk. Other sea-based classics include Homer's *Odyssey*, Daniel Defoe's *Robinson Crusoe*, Joseph Conrad's *Lord Jim* and *The Riddle of the Sands* by Erskine Childers.

Dee Caffari's tortilla pizza ⚓

British yachtswomen Dee Caffari MBE is the first woman to have sailed single-handed and non-stop around the world in both directions, and the only woman to have sailed non-stop around the world three times. Yes, three times. Like many of her fellow competing sailors she has little time for action in the galley and freeze-dried food rules – she clearly has other stuff on her mind. But the night before she leaves for a race is another matter and thoughts turn to one of her favourite foods: pizza. This is her unashamed cheat's version, using a tortilla wrap as a base, and it can be made quickly and easily on board, assuming you have an oven. If needed, the toppings can all be long-life, too.

For 2
4 wholemeal flour tortillas
4 tbsp ready-made tomato sauce
topping of your choice – chopped ham, pepperoni, tuna, mushrooms, peppers
2 or 3 fistfuls of ready-grated cheese (mozzarella or Cheddar)

Preheat the oven to 200°C/fan 180°C/gas 6. Using the tortilla wraps as a pizza base, place the first one on a baking tray. Spread with 1 tablespoon of tomato sauce. Sprinkle a little of the cheese over that and then add your topping. Finish with another sprinkling of cheese before placing in the oven. Bake for 5 minutes or until golden. Cut into quarters. Then start again for the next one, munching as you go.

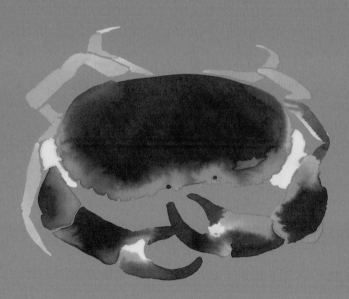

Super-quick cassoulet

An oxymoron, I know, as this south-western French speciality usually takes a couple of days to make from scratch. But now that ready-prepared duck confit is widely available, and tinned beans are a perfectly acceptable substitute to dried, a cassoulet – the mother of all pork and bean recipes – is within reach of the boater. And it's just so utterly right for a cold day on the water.

For 4

4 Toulouse or other garlicky sausages

1 x 800g tin duck confit (containing 2 legs), fat scraped off (reserving 1 tbsp), skin removed, and meat cut into small pieces

100g smoked lardons or cubed pancetta

1 large onion, peeled and chopped

3 garlic cloves, peeled and crushed

1 x 400g tin tomatoes

1 tbsp Dijon mustard

1 bouquet garni

1 x 400g tin beef consommé

2 x 400g tins haricot beans, drained and rinsed

handful of flat-leaf parsley, chopped

salt and pepper

Grill the sausages until cooked, set aside and keep warm. Heat the tablespoon of duck fat in a large pan, add the lardons or pancetta and brown for a couple of minutes. Turn the heat down, stir in the onion and garlic and soften gently for 5 minutes. Add the drained tomatoes, confit duck, mustard, bouquet garni, beef consommé and beans. Simmer for 20 minutes, uncovered, then cut the sausages into chunks and add to the pan. Season, stir in the chopped parsley and serve.

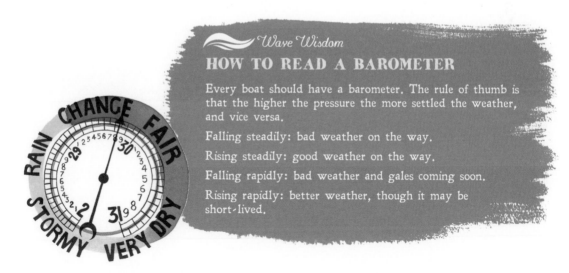

Wave Wisdom
HOW TO READ A BAROMETER

Every boat should have a barometer. The rule of thumb is that the higher the pressure the more settled the weather, and vice versa.

Falling steadily: bad weather on the way.

Rising steadily: good weather on the way.

Falling rapidly: bad weather and gales coming soon.

Rising rapidly: better weather, though it may be short-lived.

Posh beans on toast

I could eat these for lunch every day of the week. The addition of mustard, capers and anchovies gives this dish a satisfying meatiness and an impressive depth of flavour, and owes more than a nod to the classic Italian pasta sauce puttanesca – the store-cupboard supper of choice for ladies of the night, so the story goes.

For 4
2 tbsp olive or rapeseed oil
1 medium onion, peeled and chopped
2 garlic cloves, peeled and crushed
1 x 400g tin chopped tomatoes
2 x 400g tins cannellini or haricot beans, drained
4 anchovy fillets, chopped (optional)
1 tbsp capers, rinsed
2 tbsp black olives, pitted and chopped
1 tsp Dijon mustard
handful of basil leaves, torn
½ tsp ground cumin
4 thick slices sourdough, toasted
salt and pepper

To serve:
Parmesan cheese, freshly grated

Heat the oil in a large saucepan and soften the onion and garlic. Add the tomatoes, beans, anchovies, capers and olives, and simmer uncovered for 10 minutes or so until the mixture thickens. Add the mustard, basil, cumin and seasoning. Serve over toast and top with the grated cheese, or alternatively stir into pasta for a carb fest.

Instant fondue

Cue Vacherin. This Swiss/French cows' milk cheese, found mainly in the Jura region, is in season from October to April and comes in a round box made of spruce, which can be put straight into the oven. Scoop out the molten cheese with crusty bread or boiled baby new potatoes. You can dress it up a bit, too, if you are in harbour – add a topping of breadcrumbs, some chopped fresh herbs (parsley is good), a handful of pine nuts and a drizzle of nut oil before baking. Camembert is a good alternative when Vacherin is out of season.

For 2 (or 4 as a starter)
1 Vacherin
2 tbsp white wine

Preheat the oven to 180°C/fan 160°C/gas 4. Wrap the bottom of the cheese box in foil, then remove the lid and sit the box (with foil) in the lid so the cheese doesn't ooze out. Cut slashes in the top of the cheese and pour the wine over, then put on a baking tray and cook for 15 minutes.

Miso, tofu and noodle soup

There's something so immensely comforting about a big steaming bowl of Japanese-style noodles – sustaining and cleansing all in one hit. You can buy sachets of pre-cooked noodles in most supermarkets, but if you can't find them just cook some normal dried noodles beforehand. And tofu is a bit of a star on board as the little boxes store happily for months. This soup takes minutes to make yet delivers much on the flavour front. If you can't find pak choi use asparagus instead, or use both if you want to increase your vegetable intake.

For 2
700ml water
2 tbsp miso paste (white miso is best, otherwise a good brand of red miso)
1 carrot, peeled and cut into matchsticks
200g pak choi, bulb end trimmed and sliced
4 spring onions, trimmed and sliced
2 x 150g sachets udon noodles
300g packet silken firm tofu, cut into 2cm cubes

Bring the water to the boil in a large, deep saucepan. Add the miso paste and stir until dissolved. Reduce the heat. Add the carrots and pak choi and simmer for 2 minutes. Add the spring onions and simmer for another minute. Add the noodles and heat through. Serve in deep soup bowls and top with the tofu.

Cappelletti and spinach soup

This is a complete cheat as all the ingredients are ready-prepared, but it tastes good, uses only one pot, and takes under 10 minutes from start to finish. I use the smaller, fresh ravioli called cappelletti, as they take only 4 minutes to cook – there are many different pasta fillings out there so take your pick, but the meaty ones seem to work best. You can use plain passata, but the ones that come with vegetables make the taste even better.

For 4
700g tomato passata
1 litre water
300g cappelletti
250g spinach leaves, washed and ready to eat

To serve:
Parmesan cheese, grated
salt and pepper

Put the passata in a saucepan with the water and bring to the boil. Add the cappelletti and cook following the instructions on the packet. One minute before the pasta has finished cooking, tip in the spinach leaves and cover. When the spinach has wilted, season and serve the soup with the grated Parmesan.

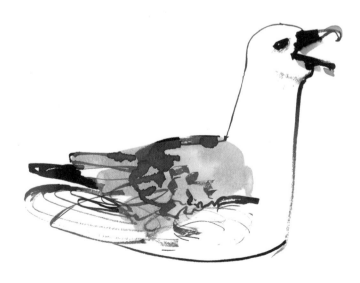

TEN GREAT UK LOCATIONS TO DROP ANCHOR

STUDLAND BAY, DORSET
On a summer's day you could be in the Caribbean, such is the often-turquoise water and long, soft, sandy beach. Watch out for naturists.

OSBORNE BAY, ISLE OF WIGHT
Until recently, this stretch of coast near East Cowes was inaccessible to the public – welcome to Queen Victoria's summer place, Osborne House.

NEWTOWN CREEK, ISLE OF WIGHT
Also known as Newtown River, it's the island's only National Nature Reserve and is made up of several estuaries that teem with wildlife – a birdwatcher's paradise.

HELFORD RIVER, CORNWALL
Like being in a Daphne du Maurier novel. It's one of the most unspoiled areas in the region, with its deep sheltered valleys, ancient oak forests and hidden creeks.

BEAULIEU RIVER, HAMPSHIRE
Flowing through the (very old) New Forest into the Solent, it's 12 miles long and entirely owned by the local lord, Montagu of Beaulieu.

KYLES OF BUTE, SCOTLAND
A dramatic, narrow sea channel which separates the Isle of Bute from the Cowal Peninsula on the Scottish mainland.

STRANGFORD LOUGH, COUNTY DOWN
The largest sea lough in the British Isles, and virtually landlocked, apart from the route through Strangford Narrow to the Irish Sea.

RIVER CONWY, NORTH WALES
It's 27 miles long from its source to Conwy Bay, with its World Heritage Site castle and two famous bridges. Salmon and sea trout abound.

ST MARY'S, ISLES OF SCILLY
The largest of the five inhabited Isles of Scilly (and dozens more uninhabited), an archipelago off the Cornish coast, with sweeping sea views and rugged coastlines.

PEEL, ISLE OF MAN
It's the third largest town after Douglas and Ramsay, but is often called the only city as it boasts the island's cathedral. It's also a busy fishing port.

Smoked salmon, beetroot and horseradish salad

This salad couldn't be much easier, or prettier. Add some boiled potatoes to the crème fraîche dressing to make the meal more substantial.

For 4

8 ready-cooked beetroot, cut into quarters
1 shallot, peeled and finely chopped
2 tsp balsamic vinegar
2 tbsp olive or rapeseed oil
170ml crème fraîche
1 tbsp freshly squeezed lemon juice
1 tbsp horseradish sauce
200g sliced smoked salmon
few sprigs of dill
salt and pepper

Combine the beetroot with the shallot, balsamic vinegar, oil, salt and pepper. In another bowl, mix together the crème fraîche, lemon juice and horseradish sauce. To serve, divide the beetroot mixture between four plates, top with the sliced smoked salmon, spoon the horseradish dressing around, and top with a few sprigs of dill.

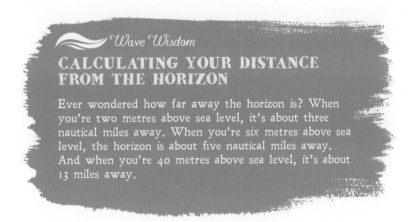

Wave Wisdom

CALCULATING YOUR DISTANCE FROM THE HORIZON

Ever wondered how far away the horizon is? When you're two metres above sea level, it's about three nautical miles away. When you're six metres above sea level, the horizon is about five nautical miles away. And when you're 40 metres above sea level, it's about 13 miles away.

Shirley Robertson's avocado and jalapeño hot dogs ☀

Shirley Robertson OBE made it into the history books by becoming the first British woman to win two Olympic gold medals at consecutive games, first in Sydney in 2000, and then in Athens in 2004. An Isle of Wight resident, these days she is just as likely to be seen in front of the camera presenting CNN's monthly sailing programme, *Mainsail*. So what does Shirley like to eat on board? She's rather partial to a hot dog. And she's not alone – there's a hot dog revival going on, from Los Angeles to London. Not the sort you get on street corners after a football match, but superior, handmade dogs, served in specially baked rolls with imaginative extras. While most of us don't have access to these superior bangers, we can take inspiration from the trend. Seek out shrink-wrapped hot dogs rather than tinned ones (they seem to taste better), then drop into a Thermos full of boiling water until you are ready to eat.

For 4
4 jumbo frankfurters
4 hot dog buns
2 ripe avocados, peeled and sliced
4 tbsp sour cream or crème fraîche
pickled jalapeños, to taste
4 tbsp Mexican salsa (hot)

Heat the dogs according to packet instructions. Split the rolls and start layering: first the avocado slices, then a tablespoon of sour cream on each, followed by jalapeños to taste, a hot dog each, and finally the salsa.

Pasta e ceci

That's pasta and chickpeas – a perfect boat dish if ever there was, thanks to the abundance of tins and quick preparation. This Roman *cucina povera* classic couldn't be more rustic, but it will warm the cockles on a cold day and keep you going until dinner. You can use pancetta in place of the chopped anchovies if you prefer, and you can bump up the vegetable quota with chopped onions, carrots and celery. It's also good with borlotti beans. Instead of grated Parmesan, you can finish each serving with a few drops of the best extra virgin olive oil – or even better, use both.

For 4

2 tbsp olive or rapeseed oil

2 garlic cloves, peeled and crushed

1 sprig of fresh rosemary, leaves chopped, or 1 tsp dried rosemary, crumbled between your fingers

4 anchovy fillets, chopped

2 x 400g tins chopped tomatoes

2 x 400g tins chickpeas, rinsed and drained

500ml water

100g angel hair (thin) spaghetti

salt and pepper

To serve:

extra virgin olive oil

Parmesan or pecorino cheese, freshly grated (optional)

Heat 1 tablespoon of oil in a saucepan over a medium heat. Add the garlic and rosemary and cook, stirring, for a minute. Add the anchovies, crushing them down, and cook for a minute more, until 'melted'. Add the tomatoes, chickpeas and water and simmer for 10 minutes. Break the pasta into pieces and add to the pot, then cook uncovered for 3 minutes until it is al dente. Turn off the heat, season and let it sit for a few minutes before serving with a slick of your best olive oil, and/or the grated cheese.

Lamb with sumac and butter-bean mash

This is as complicated as Sunday lunch gets on the boat. Instead of roasties, there are mashed garlicky beans lifted with fresh coriander, and instead of a joint, succulent chops with an aromatic rub – and all without spending too long at the stove.

For 4
8 lamb loin chops
2 tbsp olive or rapeseed oil
4 tsp sumac, plus extra to serve
3 garlic cloves, peeled and crushed
2 x 400g tins butter beans, drained and rinsed
125ml water
2 tsp vegetable bouillon powder (or a vegetable stock cube, crumbled)
handful of coriander, chopped
salt and pepper

Preheat the grill to high. Rub oil over each chop, season with salt and pepper and sprinkle with sumac, rubbing in the spice with your fingers. Grill the chops for 10–15 minutes, turning once, depending on the thickness of the chops and how you like to eat them. As the chops cook, soften the garlic in the remaining oil in a saucepan for a couple of minutes, then add the beans and water, sprinkle the bouillon over and simmer for 5 more minutes. Roughly mash the beans with a fork and stir in the chopped coriander. Serve with the chops.

Four recipes for your pressure cooker

No. 1: Sir Robin Knox-Johnston's spicy dhal ☸

Sir Robin Knox-Johnston loves his pressure cooker (see page 13). A legendary British yachtsman, he was the first person to sail single-handed and non-stop around the world in 1968 and has been declared the UK's Yachtsman of the Year no fewer than three times, finally receiving a tap on the shoulder from Her Majesty the Queen in 1995. RKJ, as he is often referred to, also loves a curry, and this fiery dhal warms him up in an instant. If you don't have the list of spices to hand, you could just use a couple of teaspoons of ready-blended curry powder. And if you want to cook this without pressure, simmer with a lid for 30 minutes.

For 4
1 tbsp rapeseed oil
1 onion, peeled and chopped
2 garlic cloves, peeled and chopped
2 tsp ground cumin
2 tsp ground coriander
1 tsp crushed dried chillies
½ tsp mustard seeds
500g red lentils
1.2 litres water
1 tsp garam masala
salt and pepper

To serve:
handful of coriander, chopped (optional)
1 onion, peeled, sliced and fried (optional)
boiled basmati rice or toasted wholemeal pitta bread

Heat the oil in the pressure cooker and soften the onion and garlic. Add the spices and cook for a minute or two. Add the lentils and water. Secure the lid and bring up to full pressure, then reduce the heat to medium and cook for 5 minutes. Turn off the heat and vent immediately (the dhal should be quite soupy). Stir in the garam masala and add the chopped coriander and/or fried onions, if you are using them, then season. Serve with rice or toasted, split, wholemeal pitta bread.

No. 2: Ratatouille

Who needs meat when vegetables taste this good? And this really is a matter of chucking it all in. I wouldn't bother doing this on the boat unless I was using a pressure cooker. At home, I leave this in a slow oven for 45 minutes. Add a couple of chopped green or red peppers if you like. Eat on its own with crusty bread, or serve as a side dish with grilled meat or fish.

For 4

750g aubergine, cut into 3cm cubes
500g courgette, cut into 2cm slices
1 large onion, peeled and chopped
1 x 400g tin chopped tomatoes
5 garlic cloves, peeled and chopped
1 tsp dried herbes de Provence, or thyme
2 bay leaves
½ tsp crushed dried chillies
3 tbsp extra virgin olive or rapeseed oil
handful of basil leaves, torn
salt and pepper

Put all the ingredients, except 2 tablespoons of the oil and the basil, into the pressure cooker. Secure the lid and bring up to pressure. Turn the heat down to medium and cook for 6 minutes. Turn off the heat and vent immediately. When you are ready to serve, stir in the remaining oil and the basil, and season. Good warm or at boat temperature.

No. 3: Lamb and artichoke tagine with lemon couscous

A Moroccan tagine is made for pressure-cooking, with its slow-cooked meat, dried fruits and vegetables. But not everybody likes the fruit and meat thing, so here's one with artichokes and peas – perfect for spring and summer. The secret ingredient here is ras el hanout. This amazingly complex, aromatic spice mix, with its dried rose-petals, lavender and cloves, elevates this lamb stew to another level, and is now available at a supermarket near you (if you can't find any then use your own Spice Mix No. 1, see page 17). Sometimes I scatter toasted almond flakes over the couscous. If you want to cook this stew in the conventional way, then simmer for an hour and a half on the hob before adding the peas and artichokes and heating through.

For 4

2 tbsp olive or rapeseed oil
1 onion, peeled and chopped
3 garlic cloves, peeled and crushed
500kg diced lamb leg
4 tsp ras el hanout spice mix
700ml water
300g ready-shelled garden peas (or tinned peas, drained)
1 x 400g tin artichoke hearts, drained
handful of fresh mint, chopped
250g couscous
grated zest of 1 lemon
salt and pepper

Heat 1 tablespoon of the oil in the pressure cooker and add the onion, garlic, lamb and spice mix, then brown the lamb, uncovered, for 5 minutes, stirring frequently. Add the water, secure the lid, then bring up to pressure and cook for 20 minutes. Release the pressure and add the peas, artichokes and mint (keeping back a tablespoon of mint for the couscous). Heat through without pressure (lid off) for 5 minutes, then season.

Meanwhile, place the couscous in a large bowl with 400ml of boiling water and 1 tablespoon of oil. Stir, cover with clingfilm and stand for 5 minutes. Add the grated lemon zest, season and stir before topping with the remaining fresh mint and serving with the tagine.

No. 4: A good beef stew

The pressure cooker really comes into its own here, reducing that 3-hour conventional cooking time to a mere 30 minutes. It's basically a French daube – so if you want to be more Provençal about it, then add a sliver of orange peel in with the meat.

For 4

1 tbsp olive or rapeseed oil

1 onion, peeled and chopped

1 head of garlic, cloves separated, skins left on

100g smoked lardons or cubed pancetta

2 tsp flour

1 x 400g tin chopped tomatoes

500ml red wine

100ml water

1 bouquet garni (or 2 bay leaves and 1 tsp dried thyme)

1 kg braising beef, cut into 3cm pieces

4 carrots, peeled, chopped in half and split lengthways

salt and pepper

Heat the oil in the bottom of the pressure cooker, add the onion, garlic and lardons, and fry gently for 10 minutes until the onions soften and the lardons start to brown. Stir in the flour and cook for a couple of minutes. Add the tomatoes, wine, water, herbs and beef, then season. Clamp on the lid. Bring up to full pressure, turn the heat down to medium and cook for 25 minutes. Turn off the heat and let the steam vent. Add the carrots, bring up to full pressure, and cook for a further 5 minutes before letting the steam vent. Serve with buttery mashed potatoes or crusty bread.

Salted caramel and banana crunch

Anyone who likes banoffee pie will love this quick, rather messy dessert. Salted caramel is addictive and everywhere. I'm not suggesting you start boiling up condensed milk to make your caramel sauce on board, rather that you buy a jar of ready-made supermarket sauce (Marks and Spencer does a salted toffee sauce that works just fine). A small serving goes a long way, but if you're really in need of a big sweet hit then just double the quantities.

For 4
130g salted caramel sauce
150ml extra thick Greek yoghurt
5 digestive biscuits
2 bananas, sliced
mint (optional)

Mix the salted caramel sauce with the yoghurt in a bowl. Crush the biscuits in a plastic bag (using a bottle of wine, or whatever weight you have to hand). Divide half the crushed biscuits between four tumblers, followed by half the banana slices, then dollop over half the salted caramel mixture. Repeat, saving a few crumbs to scatter on top, along with some mint leaves.

THE BEAUFORT SCALE

One man's stiff breeze... might be another man's gentle puff. Cue the Beaufort scale, devised in 1805 by a Royal Navy Officer, Sir Frances Beaufort, to measure wind speed on sea and land. A less precise measurement than, say, a watt, it was rather a way of recording the wind for Nelson's navy. Beaufort used the effects of the wind, rather than a description of the wind itself, so 'a gale' became Storm Force 10 – 'that which no canvas can withstand', choosing the billowing sails of a man-of-war as his point of reference, something the Navy could easily understand. It's still in use today, most notably in the familiar, soothing rhythms of the shipping forecast on BBC Radio 4. The scale ranges from the millpond of a Force 0 to the mayhem of a Force 12.

Hedgerow brûlée

Late summer means wild blackberries. Our hedgerows are bursting with them. Pick them in the morning and eat later as a sun-ripened treat on the boat. This is a great way of serving blackberries, or indeed any berries – a twist on classic crème brûlée. I've used extra thick double cream to avoid any whipping, but you could also use full-fat Greek yoghurt.

For 4
400g wild blackberries, washed
300ml extra thick double cream
2 tbsp caster sugar

Preheat the grill to hot. Divide the blackberries between 4 metal ramekins, then dollop on the cream, smoothing it down with the back of a spoon. Scatter the caster sugar over and place the ramekins under the grill for 3–4 minutes, until the sugar forms a golden crust. Serve.

she sells sea shells on the seashore

At Home

The sun is shining, there's a gentle breeze, and a day or weekend on the water beckons. Now if you're anything like me – and if you're reading a cookbook then you probably are – you're also thinking about your stomach. Namely, what delicious morsels are going to be enjoyed on board today?

It's about the sailing, yes, but it's also about the eating (and drinking). And you don't want to spend too long in the galley when everyone around you is enjoying the sun and the surf, so with a little bit of thinking and cooking ahead you can enjoy both – and take all the glory.

To fit in with the ethos of this book – that is, spending a minimum of time at the stove – these recipes are as straightforward as those to be cooked on board. They might just require a little more kit than there is on the boat, and they might spend longer in the oven. Baked goods rule, from brownies to flapjacks.

I've lately become more than a little obsessed with frittata, which is the perfect make-ahead boat food. It uses up leftovers, can be made with many different ingredients, transports easily, and contains no pastry – a bonus in this healthier age. Serve it with a crunchy green salad and a crisp white wine and that's one stellar boat lunch.

And if I had to pick the ultimate boat cake – you've got to have a boat cake – it would be fruitcake. It lasts for ages and is packed with fruit and nuts, which keeps you going (and keeps you regular) for days. Enjoy.

Honey, blueberry and pecan granola

This is so easy to make and half the price of shop-bought granola, and it's a great boat staple as its uses go way beyond breakfast. Scatter over grilled peaches or other fruit with a dollop of crème fraîche for extra crunch and sweetness, or just grab a handful to keep energy levels up mid-sail. Mix and match with different nuts and fruit, too – I love goji berries or ready-to-eat prunes – and use any combination of nuts that you have to hand. It should keep two of you going for a week for breakfast.

200g pecan nuts, roughly chopped
450g jumbo oats
200g mixed seeds (sunflower, linseed, pumpkin)
150ml extra virgin rapeseed oil
125ml runny honey
100g dried blueberries

Preheat the oven to 180°C/fan 160°C/gas 4. In a large bowl, thoroughly mix together the nuts, oats, seeds, rapeseed oil and honey. Tip the mixture into a large roasting tin and bake for 15–20 minutes or until golden, stirring frequently so it toasts evenly (watch it like a hawk – a minute too long and it's over-roasted). Remove from the oven and leave to cool. Stir in the blueberries and scoop into a storage jar. Serve with natural yoghurt or milk and fresh berries.

TEN GREAT BOATING FILMS

Master and Commander: The Far Side of the World (2003, Peter Weir)

Titanic (1997, James Cameron)

The Perfect Storm (2000, Wolfgang Petersen)

Mutiny on the Bounty (1962, Lewis Milestone)

Moby Dick (1956, John Huston)

Dead Calm (1989, Phillip Noyce)

White Squall (1996, Ridley Scott)

Lifeboat (1944, Alfred Hitchcock)

The Old Man and the Sea (1958, John Sturges)

Captain Horatio Hornblower (1951, Raoul Walsh)

Pumpkin, pine nut and Parmesan tart

Come the autumn, when squash and pumpkin are abundant, my recipes gravitate towards the sweet, orange-fleshed vegetables. An American Thanksgiving classic, pumpkin pie is hard to beat but oddly jarring to the British palate – we tend to like our squash dishes savoury. So with that in mind I've created this version and haven't looked back, taking full advantage of the conveniences that its sweeter cousin enjoys by using time-saver (Libby's) tinned pumpkin purée. Serve with a crisp, green salad.

For 4
250g ready-rolled shortcrust pastry, chilled
1 tbsp butter
1 medium onion, peeled and finely chopped (preferably in a food processor)
2 large free-range eggs
425g tin pumpkin purée
150g Parmesan cheese, freshly grated
40g pine nuts, lightly toasted
340ml evaporated milk
salt and pepper

Roll out the pastry and line a 25cm loose-bottomed tart tin with it. Leave to chill for 20 minutes. Preheat the oven to 200°C/fan 180°C/gas 6. Blind bake the pastry for 15 minutes and set aside. Turn down the oven to 180°C/fan 160°C/gas 4. Melt the butter in a saucepan, add the onion and soften until translucent. Beat the eggs in a large bowl. Add the pumpkin purée, softened onion, Parmesan and pine nuts and combine. Stir in the evaporated milk and season. Tip into the pastry case and cook for 30 minutes, or until set. Leave to cool a little before turning out. Serve warm or at room temperature.

Wave Wisdom

HOW TO SMOKE A FISH

The magical combination of salt and smoke is one of the oldest ways of imparting flavour and preserving protein, and it couldn't be easier – you just need a bit of kit to get started. For that, turn to www.hotsmoked.co.uk, who will supply all your smoking needs, from the basic to the state-of-the-art. I use a (basic) Camerons Gourmet Mini Smoker, which fits neatly on my home gas hob, or on the barbecue, and will hot smoke two decent-sized mackerel. Or if you want to preserve your fish for up to three weeks, go for a cold smoker, which is equally easy to use.

First scatter salt (I use Maldon sea salt, but cheaper table salt is fine) over a non-metallic plate, place the fish fillets on top and scatter with another layer of salt. Leave for between 5 and 50 minutes, depending on the thickness of the fillets (small mackerel fillets take 5–10 minutes, trout fillets take about 12 minutes) and the salt that you decide to use. Then rinse off under the cold tap and pat dry with kitchen towel. Now you're ready to smoke. I use hickory and alder wood grains, but my mate on the Isle of Wight (funk soul legend Mark King), who first inspired me to start smoking, uses oak and apple wood (see his wife's recipe for smoked mackerel kedgeree on page 55). As soon as it starts to smoulder, turn the heat down and place your fish on the rack, cover and smoke until ready, about five to ten minutes – just remember to keep your windows open.

Hot-smoked salmon and horseradish pâté

Salmon pâté comes in many guises, but however much you play around with it the simplest combination always seems to be the best: salmon (or trout), cream cheese and lemon. I've added a spoonful of horseradish sauce for an extra kick, but you can omit this if you prefer. I use hot-smoked fillets, but poached salmon works well, too. Eat with fresh bread or toast, and a cucumber salad: halve a cucumber lengthways, scoop out the seeds with a teaspoon, slice, then season, dress with oil and vinegar and scatter with some chopped fresh dill.

For 4, as a starter
180g hot-smoked skinless salmon fillets
100g cream cheese
grated zest and juice of 1 lemon
1 tbsp horseradish sauce
salt and black pepper

Put all the ingredients in a bowl, being generous with the black pepper, and mash together with a fork. Add more lemon juice to taste, and tip into a storage jar (I use a glass Le Parfait jar). Chill for a few hours or overnight in the fridge to let the flavours mingle and serve straight from the jar.

Asparagus and goats' cheese frittata

The perfect picnic and boat food, easily portable frittatas are a handy way to use up leftovers and will deliver a good-looking centrepiece for a summery lunch. Instead of asparagus, try using ready-roasted red peppers.

For 4

1 tbsp olive or rapeseed oil

1 leek, trimmed, washed and thinly sliced

8 large free-range eggs, beaten lightly and seasoned

1 bunch of asparagus, woody part of the stems removed, cooked until just tender, and sliced

handful of flat-leaf parsley, chopped

200g goats' cheese, crumbled

Heat the oil over a medium heat in a heavy-bottomed non-stick frying pan, add the leek and soften. Add the eggs to the pan along with the asparagus and parsley and top with the cheese. Cook gently until the bottom is set, about 10 minutes. Meanwhile, heat the grill. Remove the pan from the hob and place under the grill until the egg is set and the top is lightly browned. Serve warm or at room temperature, cut into slices.

Chorizo and chestnut sausage rolls

I tried these out one Christmas when I had some leftover chestnuts, and I've been making them all year round ever since – they make a particularly delicious, if rather wicked, boat snack. The sweetness of the chestnuts and the salty, spicy chorizo are perfect bedfellows. I make them smaller than your average sausage roll: in-the-mouth-in-one means fewer crumbs on the boat. You can make this entirely with chorizo, but I like to use a combination of classic pork bangers and chorizo (the fresh kind). Or you can use just classic pork bangers – the best you can find.

Makes 30 sausage rolls
200g best pork sausages, skins removed
200g fresh chorizo sausages, skins removed
100g chestnuts (cooked and vacuum-packed), finely chopped
1 tbsp flat-leaf parsley, chopped
500g ready-made puff pastry
1 egg, beaten
salt and pepper

Preheat the oven to 200°C/fan 180°C/gas 6 and grease a baking sheet. In a bowl (a food processor is quickest), combine the sausage meat, chopped chestnuts and parsley, then season. Divide the pastry into halves and roll out into matching rectangles. Cut each rectangle into four strips, making two strips slightly wider than the other two (so you end up with four wider and four narrower strips). Shape the meat into thin sausage shapes and lay down the middle of the four narrower pastry strips. Brush the edges with the beaten egg, then lay the four wider pastry strips over the top and use a fork pressed along the edges to seal. Cut into 3cm pieces and lay on the baking sheet, then brush with more beaten egg. Cook for 15 minutes until crisp and golden before cooling on a wire rack.

FIVE GREAT (ANONYMOUS) BOATING QUOTES

'Mackerel skies and mares' tails, soon will be time to shorten sails.'

'You should return to your home port before or when the wind speed exceeds the temperature.'

'You should proceed at a speed less than the depth beneath your keel in metres.'

'The first rule for coastal cruising: start early; finish early.'

'Navigation is what tells you where you are, even when you aren't.'

Chris Galvin's red pepper and onion marmalade

This is the foundation for piperade basquaise, a Basque classic, which is one of Chris Galvin's all-time favourite dishes. Chris will whip up this marmalade regularly at his seaside home in Cowes, to be scoffed later on his yacht with scrambled eggs, crunchy croutons and slices of crispy ham.

You can buy piquillo peppers in some supermarkets, or from www.brindisa.com. The marmalade will keep happily in the fridge or cool box over the weekend and it makes a fabulous partner to a range of dishes, from sausages to grilled mackerel. The trick is to slice those onions super-thin – I use a mandolin (see page 11), but failing that a steady hand and a little longer cooking time is fine.

For 4
50ml olive oil
300g Spanish onions, peeled and finely sliced
pinch of espelette pepper (cayenne pepper or crushed chillies will do if you can't find it)
1 garlic clove, peeled and finely chopped
300g piquillo peppers, tinned or in a jar, drained and finely sliced
pinch of salt

Heat the olive oil in a wide-bottomed saucepan, then add the onion and cook it gently, uncovered. Initially the onion will release some liquid, which will evaporate. Keep on a medium to low heat for 10–15 minutes, stirring occasionally. The onion should start to colour as the sugars begin to caramelise. Be careful they don't burn on the bottom and keep stirring every few minutes. The onions should be golden brown and very soft. Add the espelette pepper, garlic and piquillo peppers to the onion and cook for a further 10 minutes. Season with a little salt, cool and tip into a container, ready to transfer to the boat.

HOW TO MAKE THE PERFECT BEACH BARBECUE

It takes a certain skill not to nuke your carefully chosen meat and fish. The grill should be treated with respect, rather than pyromaniacal disdain. There are a few basics that everyone should know and most forget:

- on shingle beaches, raise your barbecue off the pebbles to prevent the stones shattering
- never cover up hot stones with cold ones (to prevent shattering)
- choose the best charcoal you can find and wait at least 40 minutes before you start grilling, until the flames have died down and a fine white ash coats the top
- use a long-handled pair of tongs to move stuff around
- have a plant-sprayer filled with water on hand for dampening down any fat flare-ups.

To make the best of our beach barbecue, we start by grilling thick slices of sourdough rubbed with garlic and finished with extra virgin olive oil, then cook sticky, juicy, spatchcocked quail (use the chicken marinade on page 54) for the ultimate finger food. Follow with best sirloin, cooked rare, or mackerel that you've caught yourself, grilled until the skin is crisp, alongside grilled corn on the cob still in its husk, slathered in butter. Finish with foil-wrapped bananas, dark chocolate tucked into the skins, cooked on the dying embers of the barbecue.

Spicy lamb burgers with tzatziki

Fire up the beach barbecue for these spicy, juicy, fragrant burgers moistened with a slick of shop-bought garlicky tzatziki (hummus also works well). This makes four good-sized patties. You can mix these up happily at anchor, if not at home or in harbour.

For 4
1 small onion or large shallot
2 tbsp mint leaves
2 tbsp flat-leaf parsley
3 garlic cloves
500g lamb mince
1 tsp ground coriander
1 tsp ground cumin
½ tsp chilli flakes
¼ tsp ground cinnamon
2 tsp sea salt
1 tsp black pepper
olive oil, for brushing

To serve:
4 wholemeal pitta breads
1 tub tzatziki
1 lemon, to squeeze

Blitz the onion, mint, parsley and garlic in a food processor (if you don't have one, just chop them finely). Turn into a bowl and mix with the remaining burger ingredients. Shape into patties and brush with olive oil. Let them sit for 30 minutes or so to allow the flavours to combine. When you are ready to eat, heat the chargrill pan or barbecue, then cook for 3–5 minutes on each side. Meanwhile, warm the pitta breads either under the grill or on the barbecue, then split open. Slather the insides with the tzatziki and slide in the burgers, giving them a quick squeeze of lemon before eating. Serve with a salad.

Cranberry, orange and pumpkin seed flapjacks

A day out on the water isn't complete without a flapjack. There's a vague nod to nutrition with its oats, seeds and dried fruit, but the butter and sugar pretty much undo all the good. Not that I'm complaining – it's a welcome burst of energy, and this recipe is my favourite of all flapjack flavour combinations. There's something about that buttery hit combined with a tang of sour cranberry, fragrant orange zest and toasted pumpkin. If you're wondering why I've used two kinds of oats, it's because they hold together better (fewer crumbs on board) and add an extra level of texture. The flapjacks keep for a few days in an airtight container and freeze happily, too.

Makes 12

250g unsalted butter
75g light soft brown sugar
6 tbsp golden syrup (heat the spoon with hot water before using so the syrup slides off more easily)
pinch of salt
200g quick-cook oats
250g jumbo rolled oats
100g dried cranberries
100g pumpkin seeds
grated zest of 2 oranges

Preheat the oven to 180°C/fan 160°C/gas 4 and line a 28 x 22cm baking tin with baking parchment. Melt the butter in a pan with the sugar, syrup and a pinch of salt. Stir well to combine, then take off the heat and stir in the oats, cranberries, pumpkin seeds and orange zest. Press evenly into the tin and bake for 25 minutes until set and golden. Mark out into squares soon after you remove the tin from the oven, before allowing the flapjacks to cool completely in the tin.

Chocolate and roasted hazelnut brownies

You've got to have a boat brownie. And these are quick to make and even quicker to eat. Make sure you use the correct size baking tin and don't overcook them. Soon after the smell starts wafting around the kitchen, they're pretty much done. Store in an airtight container and they'll keep for a few days.

100g hazelnuts
250g unsalted butter
250g dark chocolate, minimum 70% cocoa solids, broken into pieces
4 large free-range eggs
350g granulated sugar
2 tsp vanilla extract
160g plain flour
1 tsp salt

Preheat the oven to 180°C/fan 160°C/gas 4 and line a 34 x 25cm baking tin (at least 6cm deep) with baking parchment. Dry roast the hazelnuts for 5 minutes, then place in a tea towel and rub off the skins before roughly chopping the nuts. Melt the butter and chocolate together in the microwave (3 minutes on full power) or in a heatproof bowl over a saucepan of gently simmering water. Meanwhile, beat the eggs, sugar and vanilla extract together in a mixer until the mixture is thick and creamy.

Once the butter and chocolate have melted, remove from the heat, stir until combined and let cool a little before folding into the egg mixture. Sift the flour and salt together, then fold that into the mixture, along with the chopped roasted hazelnuts.

Tip into the baking tin, making sure it is evenly spread, and put in the oven for 25–30 minutes, or until the top has formed a light brown crust that has started to crack – you want it to be still gooey on the inside. Leave to cool for 30 minutes before cutting into squares while still in the tin (I would transport them in the tin, too). Peel away from the baking parchment and serve.

Apricot, date and walnut tea bread

I love tea bread. The great thing about it is that it keeps for a few days – that's if you can last that long without scoffing the lot as soon as it comes out of the oven. This one, inspired by a recipe from Diana Henry, is packed with apricots, dates, seeds and nuts, and provides a welcome energy boost.

150g stoned dates
100g ready-to-eat apricots
100ml apple juice
50ml water
175g butter
grated zest of 1 lemon
125g light brown muscovado sugar
1 large free-range egg, beaten
225g plain white flour
1 tsp baking powder
¼ tsp ground cloves
½ tsp ground ginger
1 tsp ground cinnamon
1 tsp ground nutmeg
100g walnuts, roughly chopped
1 tbsp pumpkin seeds
1 tbsp sunflower seeds

Preheat the oven to 180°C/fan 160°C/gas 4 and grease a 22 x 12 x 6cm non-stick loaf tin with butter. Blitz the dates and apricots in a food processor until finely chopped. Put them in a saucepan with the apple juice and water. Bring to the boil and simmer gently for 10 minutes, which should leave you with a sticky mush. Leave to cool. Melt the butter and allow that to cool, too, then add it to the date mixture, along with the lemon zest, sugar and egg, stirring until well combined. Sift the flour into a mixing bowl, and add the baking powder, ground spices, walnuts and seeds. Stir into the date mixture until thoroughly combined. Transfer to the loaf tin and bake for 1 hour. Leave to cool in the tin for 10 minutes, and then turn out on to a wire rack. To serve, cut into slices and eat smothered with butter. To store, wrap tightly in foil.

Chocolate fruitcake

Can you see what I've done here? I've taken a classic fruitcake and added some dark chocolate. No excuse, I love chocolate and it works, I promise – along with another surprise ingredient: a moistening drop of stout. You will need to soak the fruit 24 hours ahead, and if you keep feeding the finished cake with brandy it will see you through a month or more. Come November, when the sailing season tails off, it makes an appearance once again as Christmas cake. I've kept the mixture pretty chunky – I love coming across generous nubs of chocolate – but use a food processor to chop the prunes, walnuts and chocolate more finely if you would prefer a smoother texture.

250g stoned prunes, chopped
250g raisins
100g mixed peel
150ml brandy, rum or whisky
275g unsalted butter, softened
350g muscovado sugar (preferably dark)
3 free-range eggs
200g self-raising flour
150g plain flour
1 tsp cinnamon
¼ tsp ground ginger
¼ tsp mace
100ml stout
250g dark chocolate, minimum 70% cocoa solids, smashed up a bit
150g walnuts, roughly chopped

Soak the fruit in a bowl with 100ml of the brandy for 24 hours before you start cooking, covering the bowl tightly with clingfilm.

Preheat the oven to 170°C/fan 150°C/gas 3 and line the base of a greased 26cm springform cake tin with greaseproof paper. Cream the butter and sugar together. Add the eggs, one at a time, beating each one in thoroughly before adding the next. Sift the flours and spices and add to the mixture gradually until everything is well combined. Fold in the soaked fruit and the stout, followed by the chocolate and walnuts, and mix thoroughly. Tip into the tin and bake for 2½ hours, covering loosely with foil for the last hour or so if the top is browning too much. A skewer inserted into the centre should come out dry with a few crumbs clinging to the tip. Leave the cake to cool in the tin for 30 minutes before turning out, peeling off the paper and pricking with a skewer in a few places, then pouring the remaining brandy over.

Booze

Boating and booze go together like Wimbledon and strawberries. OK, so some may frown at the thought of alcohol on board a yacht in racing trim, but the rest of the time anything goes, and no sailor should be too proud to bring out the wine box, which you can always inflate when it's empty and use as a pillow (see my tips on page 140). Talking of wine boxes, these wines have improved a bit since the early days, so you can hold your head up high. The box also keeps the wine fresh for up to four weeks after opening, if you manage to keep your hands off it that long.

It certainly helps to know a thing or two about wine, if only to help you make a considered choice about what to put in your glass, so check out my buying tips on page 140. I know the boat is not really the place for vinous navel-gazing, but even the simplest dishes can be enhanced with the right wine choice (see page 143). Your wine tastes funny? I've also included a few helpful tips on how to spot a faulty wine (see page 142).

Let's not forget beer and cider. Buy local whenever in harbour – these days you are never far from a craft brewery or artisanal cider producer, such is their popularity.

For those of you who find that spirits are more your bag then I've included a few options, starting with the perfect gin and tonic, the boater's cocktail of choice. I've also singled out some of my favourite spirits, namely gin, whisky and rum, and shown you some fun things to do with them. I haven't forgotten those who prefer something without alcohol, and with these recipes you can play just as hard.

Buying and serving wine

Buying wine at the supermarket can feel a bit like a lucky dip, with all those unfamiliar, unpronounceable names. You're invariably better off in your local wine shop, where staff are likely to be more wine-savvy. Though if price is your main concern then the supermarkets usually triumph, such is their buying power – be careful not to get caught up by the endless special offers, though, which are more often than not the supermarket's way of shifting less interesting wines.

The good news is that it's hard to buy a bad bottle these days with today's modern vineyard and winemaking practices, and by using a few key tools to navigate your way along the shelves you will surely find something that will excite. Yes, you could single out wines wearing medals from the latest competition (little tip: bronze is really not worth shouting about), and recommendations from wine critics are a good bet if you get in there quickly before the shelves are cleared, but armed with a little knowledge, buying wine can become lots more fun.

There's no shame in a wine box. Most fall into the party-glugging category, but I've found some interesting ones – vinnaturo.com has sourced some bag-in-box wines from biodynamic and organic wine producers – I particularly love the Tempranillo, and the skin contact Trebbiano. Or reach for my favourite (5-litre) box, a Gamay called Raisins Gaulois from Beaujolais producer Marie Lapierre, available through Guildford-based www.lescaves.co.uk.

WHAT TO DO WITH YOUR EMPTY WINE BOX

Known rather charmingly as the bladder. Seek out brands that have reusable valves. Fill with water and bung in the freezer to use as an ice pack for your cool box, or as weights for your swimming-pool cover. Fill with water, poke holes in it and keep in the garden to water your plants during a dry period, or use as a camping shower. Alternatively, fill with air and use as a pillow in the bath, hot tub or on deck. Or just refill it with a better wine.

To learn more about wine, browse the web, read the guides, scour newspaper articles and attend in-store tastings (or even better, conduct your own at home). Look for familiar names and grape varieties, but be open-minded about trying new things. Stick to a budget by all means, but don't be afraid to blow it every now and again in the interests of research. And watch out for tired wines in small harbour shops – older vintages of wines meant to be quaffed young (whites and rosés particularly) will taste flat, or worse, oxidised. Seek out bin ends in specialist wine shops, and join a wine club,

such as the Wine Society – it will open up a whole world of experimentation.
Also consider buying wine online: prices are sometimes lower and the choice is invariably
greater – and you'll get access to lots of useful information, plus home delivery. And
don't forget to visit virtual wine regions for the latest vineyard updates – each major
wine-producing country usually offers a comprehensive website.

And now you've got your wine, what to drink it out of? A good glass is a must – it
can make a boring wine taste better. But as fine stemware and boats don't mix, we're
talking plastic tumblers. New Zealand manufacturer Strahl does a decent one: check
out its stemless Bordeaux and Chardonnay tumblers at www.amazon.co.uk.

Your wine doesn't smell quite right?

A lot of what you're drinking on board is probably bottled under screw cap. And that's
a good thing. Screw caps have come a long way in recent years and most large wine
producers, especially from the southern hemisphere, have embraced them. You should,
too, particularly as it makes keeping the opened wine much easier when on board. The
jury is still out on whether they're a better closure than cork for ageing wines, but for
those wines that are made to be glugged young (and that's about 95 per cent of all
the wines out there), screw-capped bottles are the way to go. The wines often taste
fresher, crisper and fruitier.

Cork, while coveted by the top châteaux, still has its problems. Your bottle smells
like damp cardboard? Well, it's probably corked. There are (unofficial) claims that up
to one in 12 bottles are corked – which means you've probably had a fair few corked
wines in your time. What does corked mean, exactly? Mould, in a word. It even has a
name: 2,4,6-trichloranisole (or TCA). Every now and then a tiny amount gets into the
cork, and the wine soaks up the smell – hence the mouldy aroma.

Your wine tastes like vinegar? That's a bad case of oxidation, then – when the wine
has been exposed to air. Bad storage is sometimes to blame, as the cork has probably
dried out.

Your wine smells of rotten eggs? That'll be the hydrogen sulphide, a sign of dodgy
winemaking. And not to be confused with a whiff of burnt matches – sulphur dioxide,
often added to freshly picked grapes and at bottling – which usually clears up when
the bottle has been open a moment or two.

White crystals? No worries, they're tartrates – natural deposits that won't harm you
or the wine. And if the wine is faulty, don't drink half of it before deciding whether it
is; just take it back to your retailer as full as possible.

How to match food and wine

The wrong choice of wine can spoil a dish completely – on land, that is. It's amazing how this thought flies out the window at sea. I once washed down a tinned beef curry with a sickly blush Zinfandel and thought it wasn't bad (I'd been swimming; it was hot). So the normal rules tend not to apply on board. That said, a few pointers will ensure that you get the most out of your boat meal.

Eating grilled fish? Then choose crunchy, fresh Picpoul de Pinet or Albariño. It's also worth noting that an acidic wine will cut through a fatty dish like a knife, making it seem less rich. It can heighten flavour, too, just like a squeeze of lemon does.

And talking of lemons, or vinegar, or any dish packed with citrus fruits, the chosen wine must have equal amounts of acidity or it will taste flat. The same applies to tomatoes: with a cooked tomato sauce, try a Chianti; for raw tomatoes, try Sauvignon Blanc.

CHILLING WINE

Temperature affects how a wine tastes. Serve a red wine too warm and it will taste jammy; serve a white wine too cold and you'll lose all those lovely fruity aromas and flavours. So bear that in mind when you leave a bottle of red out on the warm deck too long, or let a white languish in an ice-filled bucket. Use the sea as a cooling aid. Depending on the time of year, and where you are exactly, the sea offers an impromptu chill box – just secure the wine safely in a net and lower over the side (though screw-capped wines only, please, as salt water can get into the cork).

With a meat stew you can forget light Beaujolais – it simply won't stand up. But Cabernet Sauvignon? Now you're talking. The bolder the flavour of the dish, the bolder the wine must be to stand up to it.

If you do get as far as serving a sweet wine on board, then consider this: make sure the wine is at least as sweet as the food. Though, of course, there's the whole sweet-savoury thing to think about, too – a hunk of salty, tangy Stilton works well with a luscious sweet wine.

And if all you've got on board is a tannic red then forget trying to wash down a lunch of eggs, cheese or fish. Meat is the only way to go here.

There are some ingredients that just don't go with wine at all: vinegar is one, so wash your capers thoroughly. For kippers, try an Islay malt; for hot chillies, drink beer instead.

TEN GREAT BOAT FOOD AND WINE MATCHES

Game pâté and Côtes du Rhône

Barbecued quail and Pinot Noir

Oysters and Chablis

Fish and chips and Champagne

Grilled goats' cheese and Sauvignon Blanc

Pasta with sausage sauce and Chianti

Serrano (or Parma) ham and fino sherry

Salad Niçoise and Provençal rosé

Lamb chops with Rioja

Mussels and Muscadet

A QUICK GUIDE TO WINE STYLES

FOR APERITIF
Fino and manzanilla sherry, sparkling wine and Champagne, crisp, fresh fruity whites.

FOR FISH, SALADS AND PASTA
Crisp, fresh fruity whites: Chablis, Muscadet, Pinot Grigio, Soave and Sauvignon Blanc.

FOR FISHCAKES, FRITTATAS AND GRILLED CHICKEN
Smooth, dry whites: Chenin Blanc, Albariño, unoaked Chardonnay and Pinot Blanc.

FOR CRAB, LOBSTER AND KORMA
Full-flavoured whites: Roussanne, Marsanne, reserve Chardonnay and white Burgundy.

FOR LAKSA AND THAI GREEN CURRY
Aromatic whites: Riesling, Torrontés, Viognier, dry Muscat and Gewürztraminer.

FOR SALAD NIÇOISE AND SARDINES ON TOAST
Rosés: from Navarra, Provence, the Loire and Chile.

FOR PIZZA AND PÂTÉ, SALAMI AND HAM
Light, fruity reds: red Burgundy and other Pinot Noir, Beaujolais, Côtes du Rhône and Valpolicella.

FOR GRILLED MEAT, GAME AND VEGETABLES, MUSHROOMS AND CHEESE
Smooth, medium-bodied reds: Cabernet Sauvignon, Merlot, Chianti and Rioja.

FOR CASSOULET AND TAGINES, BARBECUED MEAT AND CHILLI CON CARNE
Rich, full-bodied reds: Malbec, Shiraz, Zinfandel, Fitou and Douro.

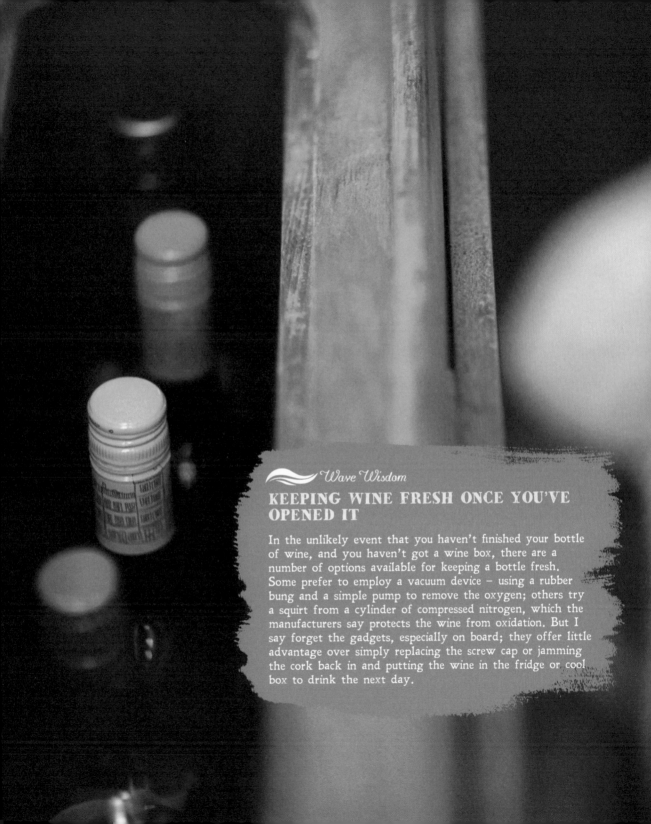

KEEPING WINE FRESH ONCE YOU'VE OPENED IT

In the unlikely event that you haven't finished your bottle of wine, and you haven't got a wine box, there are a number of options available for keeping a bottle fresh. Some prefer to employ a vacuum device – using a rubber bung and a simple pump to remove the oxygen; others try a squirt from a cylinder of compressed nitrogen, which the manufacturers say protects the wine from oxidation. But I say forget the gadgets, especially on board; they offer little advantage over simply replacing the screw cap or jamming the cork back in and putting the wine in the fridge or cool box to drink the next day.

Spirits

You're probably wondering why I've focused on just three spirits – gin, rum and (Islay) whisky – considering the whole world of booze out there. But I regard these three as essentials for the sailing community, and if I'm honest, it's what I most like to drink, particularly as the sun slips over the horizon.

Now I'm guessing that you're not likely to stock a full bar on board, so the cocktails on the following pages employ the minimum of ingredients and method but offer maximum flavour and show off these spirits at their best.

All the spirit drink recipes are for one, but as a good cocktail is all about getting the right balance, I recommend you use a jigger, the easiest, quickest method for measuring out spirits. Failing that, use a (clean) medicine cup, or an egg cup – half full is about 25ml (which is 1 shot) – or failing that use a tablespoon – 2 scant tablespoons is around 25ml. Use a measuring jug for larger quantities.

Keep a bottle of simple syrup in a cool place. You can buy it commercially, or mix it yourself: in a saucepan containing one mug of water, gradually pour and stir in one mug of granulated sugar. Heat gently until the sugar has dissolved, then bring to the boil and simmer for 2 minutes. Allow to cool, then pour into a plastic bottle, ideally straining it first to remove any undissolved crystals. It will keep for a week or two on board, or for a couple of months in the fridge.

Consider stocking a cocktail shaker in the boat locker – why not? But unless you've got a freezer on board, keep the cocktail shaking strictly for when you're in harbour with precious access to ice.

And I make no apologies for including two sour recipes – I love a sour.

Wave Wisdom

THE SOUR

An iconic cocktail, the sour evolved from the practice of adding lime juice to rum rations to prevent scurvy among sailors in the Navy during the 1700s. As fresh fruit was perishable, the juice would be doctored with rum, or gin, and later whisky, in order to preserve the juice and keep sailors healthy. And it wasn't long before they worked out that citrus fruit and spirits were enhanced by sugar. As its simplest, it's gin, rum or whisky, with lemon or lime juice, and sugar.

Gin

We can't get enough gin, it seems, such is the global craze for it. And I for one am happy. Bursting with myriad fresh, zesty, but always juniper-led flavours, it gets the tastebuds going. It remains the base of many classic cocktails, such as the martini, and it's responsible for the gimlet and the Singapore sling, which originated in the Raffles Hotel, Singapore, at the turn of the century. We'll forget for the moment that juniper-based elixirs such as gin only became widely used in Europe during the fourteenth century to ward off the Black Death, and rather remember the gin given as 'Dutch Courage' to fighting English mercenaries who went off to Holland to help out during the Thirty Years' War, doubtless bringing a few bottles back. The English embraced it, started making it, and adopted it as their own. The rest is history, as they say.

Three great gin drinks

The perfect G&T

The key ingredient in tonic, quinine, has been used against malaria for centuries, so its popularity in the British colonies, especially India, was obvious. I like Plymouth gin best, but choose your brand to suit your palate.

50ml gin
tonic water to taste
lime wedge

Pour the gin and tonic water into a tall, ice-filled glass. Run a lime wedge around the rim of the glass, squeeze and drop into the drink.

Gin and It

It's short for Gin and Italian, a reference to the sweet vermouth traditionally made in Italy, as opposed to French vermouth, which is dry.

50ml gin
25ml sweet vermouth (such as Martini Rosso)
orange wedge

Pour the gin and vermouth into an ice-filled glass and stir. Squeeze an orange wedge over the drink and drop into the glass.

Gin sour

The sour made an appearance in the first-ever cocktail book, Jerry Thomas's *Bartender's Guide*, published in 1862.

50ml gin
50ml freshly squeezed lemon juice
50ml freshly squeezed orange juice
10ml sugar syrup
½ fresh egg white
lemon wedge

Give all the ingredients except the lemon a good shaking with ice and strain into a glass. Garnish with the lemon wedge on the rim.

Whisky

Scotland and Ireland have given the world many things, but whisky is their greatest gift (spelled whiskey in Ireland, and in the USA too). The world's favourite spirit comes in many guises and every country has a different approach to making it, but it is single malt Scotch that gets whisky lovers in a froth.

The Inner Hebridean island of Islay arguably boasts the mightiest malts of them all. Here peat is all, and maturing takes place in sea-lashed warehouses which sop up the spume-laden air. The constant breeze carries a scent of brine mixed with the coconut aroma of warm gorse. Add to that a whiff of peat smoke and bog myrtle, and you have some of the key aromas of the island's famous whisky, best enjoyed on its own.

Single malt lovers wouldn't dream of sullying their drink with other ingredients, so if it's a whisky cocktail you're after, then go for a blended Scotch, a rye whiskey or a bourbon, which makes a hugely versatile base spirit.

Three great whisky drinks

Whisky sour

I like an American rye whiskey in this one, such as Jim Beam. The tanginess mixes well with the citrus fruit without losing its identity.

50ml whisky
10ml fresh lemon juice
5ml sugar syrup
lemon slice

Shake the whisky, lemon juice and sugar syrup together vigorously with ice. Strain into a glass and garnish with a lemon slice.

Hot toddy

A catch-all term for warmed alcoholic drinks, the hot toddy actually dates back beyond the seventeenth century, when it was cheaper to heat your drink than your house.

50ml water
2 cloves
1 cinnamon stick
1cm piece of fresh ginger, sliced
strip of lemon peel
50ml whisky
2 tsp honey
lemon quarter
pinch of grated nutmeg

Put the water in a small pan with the spices, ginger and lemon peel and bring to a simmer. Pour the whisky into a mug and add the spice-infused water. Stir in the honey, squeeze in the juice from the lemon and sprinkle with grated nutmeg.

Whisky mac

Avoid an Islay malt – the peatiness overpowers the ginger completely. Instead choose a blended Scotch, and don't be tempted to shake as this destroys the clarity of the drink.

50ml whisky
25ml Stone's Original Green Ginger Wine, or Crabbie's Green Ginger Wine

Pour the ingredients into an ice-filled glass and lightly stir.

Rum

If any spirit sums up the sailing nation it's rum. But there are as many definitions of what constitutes rum as there are countries that make it. In a nutshell, rum is the spirit distilled from the fermented sugars derived from molasses, which is created by repeatedly boiling the fresh juice extracted from the sugar cane plant. You can thank the Spanish and Portuguese, who brought the sugar cane plant with them to the newly discovered Brazil and Caribbean islands in the early part of the fifteenth century. By the end of the seventeenth century the French, English and Dutch had developed a taste for rum and they haven't looked back.

Cue grog. Invented by Admiral Edward Vernon when he commanded the West Indies fleet in 1740, the daily allowance of half a pint of rum per man was diluted with a quart of water and issued only twice a day in an effort to stop the ship's company becoming too trashed by the afternoon watch. Not that the men were happy about it, contemptuously naming it grog. The rum rations were to last until 31 July 1970, known as Black Tot Day, when the last tot – Pusser's was the official rum – was drawn in the fleet around the globe.

It appears that the tradition lives on, however, in the form of a modern-day grog – I confess to being a huge fan of rum punch, particularly this recipe, which I extracted from a wonderful Barbadian cook, LaurelAnn Morley, who used to run my favourite restaurant on the island, The Cove. We would wash down her Bajan feasts with her nutmeg-dusted, if rather lethal, punch. But her legacy lives on as it's still my go-to rum punch recipe.

Three great rum drinks

Dark and stormy

The key to this Bermudian classic, the origins of which are rather fuzzy, is nailing the precise ratio between the tangy snap of the ginger beer and the richness of the dark rum. The addition of lime isn't authentic, but it tastes good.

50ml dark rum	Mix all the ingredients together in a tall glass and fill
75ml ginger beer	it up with ice.
15ml lime juice	

Hot buttered rum

Another toddy, hot buttered rum stems from colonial days and is still a favourite during the autumn and winter months.

1 tsp soft butter	Put the butter, sugar, vanilla and spices in the bottom of a
1 tsp brown sugar	mug and mix well. Add the rum and top up with hot water.
few drops of vanilla extract	
pinch of ground cinnamon	
pinch of grated nutmeg	
50ml dark rum	
hot water	

LaurelAnn Morley's rum punch

I could kiss LaurelAnn Morley for singing her little ditty to me one day while serving her legendary punch on the east coast of Barbados: 'One of sour, two of sweet, three of strong and four of weak.' You can use this formula for any punch, replacing water with fruit juice, if you like.

25ml fresh lime juice
50ml sugar syrup
75ml golden rum
100ml water

To serve:
Angostura bitters
pinch of grated nutmeg

Mix all the ingredients together and stir until well combined. Serve over lots of crushed ice, add a few drops of Angostura bitters and sprinkle with freshly grated nutmeg before serving.

LIFESAVER

Founded by Sir William Hillary in 1824 after witnessing the demise of dozens of ships from his home on the Isle of Man, the Royal National Lifeboat Institution (RNLI) has saved more than 140,000 lives. It's a charitable organisation, with volunteers making up 95 per cent of its staff and chugging out bravely and uncomplainingly in all weathers for anything ranging from engine failure to man-overboard.

The Yarmouth RNLI lifeboat, the *Eric and Susan Hiscock* (named after its generous benefactors), has seen a lot of action. Its volunteers don't need much prompting to regale folks with their adventures at sea, especially when oiled with their favourite tipple, devised by Yarmouth lifeboatman Guy Ashton: one measure of golden rum, six measures of still water, the juice of half a lime for each half-pint (with the limes dropped in after squeezing), and lots of ice.

Non-alcoholic drinks

Just because you're not boozing doesn't mean that you can't have fun. And you can't beat a hot toddy on a cold day – try my non-alcoholic version with good old builder's tea below. Like the boozy equivalents, the cocktails need ice, which means harbour drinking – unless you have the luxury of a freezer on board.

Seriously good hot chocolate

Good hot chocolate is a thing of beauty – and surprisingly difficult to find. Most are too sweet, and don't use good chocolate. The answer? Make it yourself. You can control the quality of chocolate, and the level of decadence (for which read double cream). I make up a big batch of the chocolate mixture in advance, blitzing the squares in a food processor at home, then mixing with cocoa powder and storing in an airtight container.

For 2
50g dark chocolate, minimum 70% cocoa solids, chopped finely
2 tsp good cocoa powder
50ml double cream
200ml whole milk (though semi-skimmed is fine)

Mix together the chopped chocolate and cocoa powder and place in a small heatproof container (I use the mug I'll be drinking it out of). Heat the cream and milk together in a small saucepan. When it's hot (taking care not to let it boil), splosh a little over the chocolate mix and stir to melt it slightly, giving it a head start. Then add the chocolate mix to the milk mix and whisk together until blended. Pour into mugs and serve.

Tea toddy

For when you want all the warming benefits of a toddy but none of the alcoholic hit.

For 2
2 tbsp honey
2 tsp lemon or lime juice
pinch of ground cinnamon
pinch of ground cloves
pinch of grated nutmeg
500ml hot tea (I sometimes use Red Bush tea as a herbal alternative)
2 lemon or lime quarters, to garnish

Put the honey, lemon juice and spices into a mug. Top with hot, freshly brewed tea and garnish with a wedge of lemon.

Three great non-alcoholic cocktails

Virgin Mary

I think I actually prefer this non-alcoholic version of the classic Bloody Mary – the Tabasco acts as both palate-cleanser and mood-lifter, especially after a heavy night.

For 4
1 litre tomato juice
2 tbsp Worcestershire sauce
1 tsp Tabasco sauce
1 lemon, quartered
celery salt and pepper to taste

Combine the tomato juice, Worcestershire sauce and Tabasco in a jug. Squeeze a lemon quarter into each glass and chuck in the rind. Top up with the juice. Season with the celery salt and pepper, and serve with extra Tabasco.

Cranberry punch

Guaranteed to get you in the festive mood, this fruity number is a thirst-slaker.

For 8 (it's a party!)
1 litre cranberry juice
1 litre pineapple juice
200ml ginger ale
200ml soda water
fresh or tinned pineapple chunks and fresh mint leaves (optional), to garnish

In a large bowl, combine the juices, ginger ale and soda water. Serve over ice, garnished with the pineapple and mint.

Mockito

The enduring popularity of the alcoholic version of this drink (the mojito) shows no sign of letting up. But there's no reason why you can't enjoy the ride if you're not boozing.

For 4
handful of fresh mint leaves
1 tsp brown sugar
500ml apple juice
4 limes, freshly squeezed
500ml soda water

In a container, bash the mint with the brown sugar for a few seconds (I use a wooden spoon). Distribute between four tall glasses. Add ice, apple and lime juice, and top up with soda water.

Acknowledgements

This book would not have been possible without the encouragement (and pot washing) from Liz Multon, Jess Cole and the team at Bloomsbury/Adlard Coles – it was a pleasure doing business with you, girls.

And a big thanks to my mentor and mate Fiona Beckett for holding my hand throughout, and to legendary chef Chris Galvin for saying such lovely things about me in the foreword, as well as kindly contributing a recipe, along with four other stellar chef mates: Angela Hartnett, Ed Wilson, Kevin Mangeolles and Judy Joo.

And blessings to you famous sailors, who also generously contributed a recipe each: Dee Caffari, Shirley Robertson, Brian Thompson, Mike Golding and Sir Robin Knox-Johnston.

It was Julian Winslow who made those recipes come to life on the page with his photographer's eye and styling flair, while Louise Sheeran and her paintbrush added to the talent with the best boat cookbook illustrations ever.

I would have been cooking until midnight without the help of two dear friends, brilliant chef Judy Joo and rock chick Ria King, whose boundless enthusiasm in the kitchen made sure that the attention to detail didn't wane. Not forgetting my husband, Mark, who happily scoffed all the leftovers and played guinea pig throughout.

I doff my hat to digforvintage.com for sourcing props to make the pages look enticing, to Alison at Blue in Yarmouth for letting me plunder her gorgeous shop for backdrops, and to the Yarmouth Harbour Master, who let us run free.

Finally, and most importantly, thanks to my parents for giving me a love of the sea, and dad, for your tinned beef curry concoctions, which drove me to write this book.

Index